I0102566

Deconstructing ScoMo

Critical Reflections on Australia's 30th Prime Minister

Rocco Loiacono PhD
Senior Lecturer,
Curtin University Law School

Augusto Zimmermann PhD
Professor of Law,
Sheridan Institute of Higher Education

Deconstructing ScoMo: Critical Reflections on Australia's 30th Prime Minister
© **Rocco Loiacono and Augusto Zimmermann 2022**

ISBN: 978-1-922717-56-6 (paperback)

All rights reserved. No part of this publication may be reproduced, stored in a retrieval system, or transmitted in any form or by any means electronic, mechanical, photocopying, recording, or otherwise, without the prior written permission of the author.

Published in Australia by Rocco Loiacono and Augusto Zimmermann and Locke Press.

Printed in Australia by InHouse Print & Design.

A catalogue record for this book is available from the National Library of Australia

CONTENTS

'Our natural unalienable rights are now presumed to be a dispensation of government, divisible by a vote of the majority. The greatest good for the greatest number is a high-sounding phrase but contrary to the very basis of our nation, unless it is accompanied by recognition that we have certain rights which cannot be infringed upon, even if the individual stands outvoted by all of his fellow citizens. Without this recognition, majority rule is nothing more than mob rule.'

Ronald Reagan, *A Time for Choosing*, October 27, 1964

FOREWORD

Poll driven politicians with their fingers on the pulse of the latest focus group results, and on nothing much else, can keep a country ticking over just fine. Well, they can as long as times are normal and things are going fairly well. In such circumstances the need is far less visible for politicians with, say, a sincere belief in freedom or in limited government or in the need to deregulate the economy and to avoid at all costs huge spending, big government policies. You see, times are good. Things are ticking along. Hence, any moderately competent managerial politician will probably do, even one with few, if any, core beliefs or deeply held fundamental values for which he or she would sacrifice the career and the chauffeur-driven limousine, or move to the backbenches. For instance, a strong willingness to fight for traditional culture policies – to fight the culture wars if you wish to put it in those terms – is hardly required unless many on the other side of politics (and on your own side for that matter) are pushing cancel culture attitudes and identity politics programs while making more and more inroads on free speech (however much they may wrap up such inroads in spurious, Jesuitical pretences that they are not doing so). But when they are pushing such barrows, and when times are decidedly not normal, then we find the virtue of the value-driven politician who will stand up to the baying ABC mob or to the public health caste or to the wall-to-wall Keynesians in Treasury. Then we rack the value of such politicians that was not all that visible in normal times.

As a native born Canadian who came to this country in 2005 I have to confess, regretfully, that the last twenty odd months of this

Covid pandemic has stunned and somewhat disillusioned me. I never saw coming just how sheep-like so many Australians would be when politicians here (and yes, in many, many other democracies) imposed the greatest inroads on our civil liberties and freedoms in the last two or three centuries. I have written extensively in various publications in Australia and overseas, and in some law review articles too, about the follies of these public policy decisions – about how Sweden and Florida got it right and how we in Australia decidedly did not get it right. Indeed, I believe that in a decade or less we will look back on this as the worst public policy failure in this country's history – because there are many other matrices of concern other than Covid deaths, ones that include deaths from all other causes, economic devastation, runaway government spending, mental health concerns, excess deaths per year (an indicia that cannot be gamed), the way in which young people bore the overwhelming brunt of the despotic, heavy-handed policies, the hammering of the private sector but indulging of the public sector, all freedom-related concerns, and more – because it will take a few years for the ruinous outcomes on these other criteria and matrices of concern to become clear. Readers can agree or disagree with me about that according to outlook. But my point here is that it is precisely at times like these that we want politicians of principle – not ones who can barely get out of bed before finding out what that day's focus group thinks. And what we have unfortunately seen here in Australia is that the vast preponderance of today's politicians in this country, at both the State and Commonwealth level, are decidedly not ones who are values and principles driven. Some would appear not to be able to act on a core value even if they devoted the bulk of their maiden speech in Parliament to talking about how important it is. Talk is cheap and easy for politicians. Walking that talk and putting the political career in jeopardy is hard. In Australia it appears overwhelmingly to be impossible for those in our political class.

And that brings me to our current Prime Minister, Scott Morrison. I have not been any great fan of the man ever since he sneeringly dismissed the value of free speech, wrongly claiming that fighting for it 'doesn't create one job, doesn't open one business, doesn't give anyone one extra hour. It doesn't make housing more affordable or energy more affordable.' Actually, that is laughably wrong as even a moment's thought would show. Open western democracies with their vibrant economies depend completely on the free exchange of views. And the obliteration of our economy caused *not* by the Covid virus itself but by the political response to it in this country shows the economic effects of ignoring freedom-concerns. That is not to say that economic concerns are the most important item in the list of the many benefits of free speech and freedom more generally – remember that Australia is now widely perceived in Britain, the US, Canada and more widely as having descended into near police state territory during this pandemic. I simply mention this claim by our Prime Minister, this 'what has free speech and freedom ever done for us' Monty Pythonesque idiocy, as one indicia of Mr. Morrison not being a politician of any obvious principles or values. Not my cup of tea, I unhesitatingly concede.

That may be why the authors of this book asked me to write this foreword. They, too, find Mr Morrison lacking. Their grievances do not overlap perfectly with mine; their gravamens are not always mine; and vice versa. But they have made a strong case worth reading. In these non-normal times I think our Prime Minister has been judged and found wanting. So do the authors of this book. We will see what the voters think in 2022.

Professor James Allan,
Garrick Professor of Law, University of Queensland
November 2021

PREFACE

This book is a collection of articles and essays published over the course of Scott Morrison's prime ministership, with the majority focussing on the years 2020 and 2021. These pieces, written in the main by Professor Augusto Zimmermann and published in various online and print outlets and edited for this book, deal not only with Scott Morrison's handling of Covid-19, but with many issues that are critically important to those who would traditionally consider themselves Liberal voters, namely: freedom of speech, religious freedom, individual liberty, fiscal discipline, the rise of China, wokeism, the climate change cult, and so on. In 2019, the "quiet Australians" placed their faith in a man who promised his government would stand for them in these matters. However, Morrison's prime ministership has seen the Liberals continue the lurch to the left that was started by Malcolm Turnbull, leaving many of these same "quiet Australians" feeling more concerned than ever about their future and their children's future. During Scott Morrison's time in office, among other things:

- there has been no action on free speech concerns;
- the country is effectively being run by the states;
- an election promise of protecting religious freedoms is yet to happen (at the time of writing);
- people are being forced to undergo a medical treatment in order to keep their jobs and livelihoods, and participate in everyday life;
- families have been forced apart missing important milestones, celebrations and deaths;

- Australia has a record debt with no roadmap in sight to repay it;
- Churches have not been allowed to congregate freely;
- small businesses are going broke at a rate not seen since the Great Depression while government and the public service continues to expand, as do public service salaries; and
- Australians have become more divided than at any time since the Vietnam War.

Thus, we feel compelled to put pen to paper and express these concerns, especially given the next federal election will soon be upon us.

The views expressed in this book are ours and do not necessarily reflect the views of either Curtin University or Sheridan Institute of Higher Education.

Rocco Loiacono and Augusto Zimmermann
October 2021

INTRODUCTION

Just Who Is ScoMo?

On August 24, 2018, Scott John Morrison won a party room ballot of the Liberal Party to become Australia's 30th prime minister. With the party having lost confidence in Malcolm Turnbull, its MPs and senators elected Morrison as a compromise candidate in a contest with then Home Affairs Minister Peter Dutton and then Foreign Minister Julie Bishop. A largely unexpected election victory in 2019, one for the "quiet Australians", to use his words, seems to have given Morrison a great deal of power within his party, similar to the way that Paul Keating's unexpected "victory for the true believers" in 1993 made him an ALP hero. Despised by the Left because he belongs to the Liberal Party, and by the Right because he has abandoned his core constituency (captured brilliantly by Reagan's political maxim "Dance with the one that brung ya"), the question must be asked: "Just who is Scott Morrison?"

To attain an answer to this question, as well as an understanding of Scott Morrison's prime ministership, one must look at his ascension to the role. It is not a typical story of one who becomes head of a government. Unlike the vast majority of our post-war prime ministers, Morrison, it seems, did not have an acute interest in politics in his youth. Sir Robert Menzies was elected president of the Student Representatives' Council and editor of the *Melbourne*

University Magazine, as well as being a prominent member of the Law Students' Society.[1]

As John Ruddick noted in detail:

> *Gough Whitlam was devouring the politics of Rome before he was ten. Malcolm Fraser joined the Liberal party at 22 and was an MP at 24. Bob Hawke joined Labor at 18 and wrote his university thesis on industrial relations. Paul Keating joined Young Labor the first day he could and was NSW Young Labor president aged 22 – John Howard was the Young Liberal equivalent aged 23. Kevin Rudd joined Labor aged 15. At 20, Julia Gillard was a campus president and joined Labor. Tony Abbott was also a campus president and a confidante of B.A. Santamaria. Malcolm Turnbull was an active student politician while working part-time as a political reporter.*[2]

And that covers prime ministers only! Of the modern day opposition leaders, Andrew Peacock was president of the Young Liberals in 1962, became president of the Victorian Liberal Party in 1965 and, at age 27, succeeded Sir Robert Menzies in the seat of Kooyong the following year.[3] Simon Crean and Kim Beazley had politics in their blood, being the sons of federal government ministers. Peter Costello, described often as "the greatest prime minister we never had", prior to being elected to the Federal Parliament was active in student politics, initially an office-bearer of the Social Democratic Students Association of Victoria, an affiliate of Young Labor.[4]

During his legal career (he graduated from Monash University with Honours), Costello represented employers in some of Australia's best known industrial relations disputes. In 1983 and 1984, he represented the National Farmers' Federation in a case against the Australasian Meat Industry Employees Union (AMIEU). The AMIEU was seeking a unit tally system to be set up in abattoirs in the Northern Territory. The dispute focussed on one abattoir,

Mudginberri, which chose to fight the AMIEU claim. Ultimately the AMIEU claim was unsuccessful. Subsequently, Costello became counsel to organisations representing small business and rose to prominence in the 1985 Dollar Sweets case, as junior counsel assisting Alan Goldberg QC, successfully representing a confectionery company involved in a bitter industrial dispute.[5] In 1986 he was a founding member of the H. R. Nicholls Society, thus being at the forefront of the argument for reform of Australia's industrial relations system, along with Howard (at that time Federal Opposition Leader).

Ruddick also alludes to the brilliant academic record of most of our prime ministers. He writes: "The other members of Club PM studied law, history, political science, philosophy, etc., but Morrison studied economic geography (huh?)."[6] Indeed, Abbott, Hawke and Turnbull were Rhodes Scholars. Menzies graduated from the University of Melbourne in 1916 with first-class honours in Law, and then went on to build a distinguished legal career, which included serving as Counsel in the *Engineers' Case* before the High Court (at age 26), which was a landmark decision on the interpretation of the Commonwealth's constitutional powers over the States.[7] After his legal career, Menzies became Attorney-General and Deputy Premier of Victoria before moving into the federal sphere.

Morrison's first job was at the Property Council.[8] From 1995 to 2000 he then held senior roles in tourism authorities. Until 2006 he was head of Tourism Australia, when he left in circumstances that, it appears, have never been fully explained.

In the early 2000s Morrison was also State Director of the New South Wales Liberal Party, interestingly at the same time as Malcolm Turnbull's unseating of then sitting member Peter King in Wentworth. As Ruddick writes:

> *The Liberal party is viewed as this awesome election-winning machine but once inside you quickly see its awesome dysfunction and how average many of its parliamentarians are. No one had*

a better view than the state director and at some point Morrison concludes, 'I reckon I could be an MP.'

The plan was to run for Mitchell but then Bruce Baird retired in Cook. No need to rehash the details of that messiest of preselections other than to add that Sam Dastyari told FM radio in 2018 that allies of Morrison met with him seeking dirt on the initial pre-selection winner. Sam says he happily coughed something up and, coincidence or not, come the next election Morrison lands in Canberra. The alleged episode suggests Morrison had Keating-style political drive.

Following the loss of the 2007 election, Peter Costello announced he wasn't running for leader. The first contest was between Brendan Nelson and Malcolm Turnbull. Nelson won 45-42. We can conclude newbie Morrison backed Turnbull because (a) they'd been mates since state director Morrison favoured Turnbull in his own messy pre-selection and (b) Nelson named a mammoth shadow ministry with over half the party room included but Morrison was excluded.[9]

In 2009, as Malcolm Turnbull's leadership was imploding over his proposal to support then prime-minister Kevin Rudd's Emissions Trading Scheme, Joe Hockey and Abbott challenged Turnbull. Ruddick alleges that, by this stage, Morrison had five or so MPs loyal to him and the night before the vote Morrison apparently told Abbott, "My bloc's voting for Malcolm unless I get immigration".[10] Abbott defeated Turnbull by one vote and Morrison got the shadow immigration job just as illegal boat arrivals were ramping up. Tough-talking Morrison soon burst onto the nightly news. However, it must be remembered that Abbott, after six months of sustained campaigning, saw off Kevin Rudd and nearly pulled off the impossible, defeating an incumbent government at an election after only one term, a feat only achieved once in the history of this country, when the Scullin government was defeated at the height of the Great Depression in 1931.

When Abbott defeated Rudd in 2013, Ruddick asserts that Major General Jim Molan, appointed by the Abbott government as special envoy for Operation Sovereign Borders, promptly stopped the boats[11] and Morrison basked in the glory. With immigration out of the news, Morrison started publicly speculating his next role would be an economic portfolio (the surest path to the Lodge is via Treasury). Around this time, as treasurer Joe Hockey was being crippled by Cabinet leaks (probably by Turnbull), Morrison called into PM Abbott's office saying, 'Hockey's got to go'.[12] Abbott, whose loyalty is one of his strongest traits, did not agree. Turnbull, who waged a continuous campaign of revenge since he was removed from the leadership in December 2009, challenged Abbott in September 2015. Ruddick states that the Morrison bloc had grown to 15, of whom 14 voted for Turnbull.[13] Morrison, with typical casuistry, could say hand on heart he voted for Abbott but in the wash-up Morrison became Treasurer in the Turnbull Government and Hockey became Ambassador to the United States. When Turnbull's leadership imploded in 2018 a seemingly surprised Morrison emerged as PM, but it's pretty obvious what happened – the Morrison bloc presumably egged on Dutton in order to destabilise Turnbull.[14]

We can think of no better way to conclude this introduction than the way Ruddick concluded his piece:

> This sketch of Morrison's rise reveals that while he has no natural interest in political ideas he is awesome at the politics of politics. November 2021 is the 40th anniversary of Margaret Thatcher's speech at the Menzies Lecture in Melbourne where she noted: 'I count myself among those politicians who operate from conviction. Consensus is the process of abandoning all beliefs, principles, values and policies in search of something in which no one believes, but to which no one objects. The process of avoiding the very issues that have to be solved, merely because you cannot

get agreement on the way ahead. What great cause would have been fought and won under the banner "I stand for consensus"?'

During a televised leaders debate in the 2019 campaign, Morrison declared, 'I'll govern from where I always have – from the middle.' Lacking any depth, Scott Morrison's guiding principle is to be a little to the right of a very left Labor party and that's delivering us two left-wing parties.[15]

The results of this have been disastrous for Australia, at so many levels.

Introduction endnotes

1   Allan William Martin, *Robert Menzies: A Life 1894-1943*, Volume 1 (Melbourne University Press, 1993), 5.

2   John Ruddick, 'Who the bloody hell are you?', *The Spectator Australia*, April 24, 2021, at https:// spectator.com.au/ 2021/04/who-the-bloody-hell-are-you/.

3   Tony Wright, Rob Sharp, David Crowe, , 'A Great Australian and Treasure: Andrew Peacock dies in the US aged 82', *Sydney Morning Herald*, April, 16, 2021, at https://www.smh.com.au/national/andrew-peacock-dies-in-the-united-states-aged-82-20210416-p57jze.html.

4   Peter Costello with Peter Coleman, (2009) *The Costello Memoirs*, Melbourne University Publishing.

5   Ibid. The case was the first time in Australia a union was made to pay common law damages to an employer for losses caused by unlawful picketing.

6   Ruddick, above n 2.

7   Martin Allan, Menzies, *Sir Robert Gordon (Bob) (1894-1978). Australian Dictionary of Biography*, (Melbourne University Press, 2000).

8   Ruddick, above n. 2.

9   Ibid.

10 Ibid.

11 See also: Michael Koziol, 'Stop the boats' architect Jim Molan is planning a new mission - to enter Parliament, *Sydney Morning Herald*, March 15, 2016, at https://www.smh.com.au/politics/federal/stop-the-boats-architect-jim-molan-is-planning-a-new-mission--to-enter-parliament-20160315-gnjaax.html#ixzz4AdKXIAjV.

12 Ruddick, above n. 2.

13 Ibid.

14 Ibid.

15 Ibid.

Part 1

FREEDOM OF SPEECH, OTHER FUNDAMENTAL FREEDOMS AND THE RULE OF LAW

With Friends Like ScoMo, Who Needs Enemies?[1]

The Australian Labor Party hasn't been the party for blue-collar battlers for a very, very long time. Instead, this is the party for group interests pushing such things as state-sanctioned abortion on demand, assisted suicide, the LGBTIQPAX+ agenda, radical environmentalism, etc.

However, in many ways the Liberal Party is not so different. According to *Legal Rights Audit*, the Morrison government has been responsible for a substantial increase in the violation of fundamental legal rights.[2] Morgan Begg, the report's main author and research fellow with the Institute of Public Affairs, writes: "The Coalition [Liberal-National] government is trashing fundamental legal rights of all Australians, creating an unprecedented challenge to individual freedom and human dignity".[3]

Professor Zimmermann has had personal experience of the problem. As Senior Vice-President of the Fremantle Division of the WA Liberal Party, he was deeply happy to see an important motion which was proposed by distinguished member and Fellow of the IPA, Sherry Sufi, being approved by the WA Liberal Party. It read as follows:

> *That the Liberal Party of Australia (WA Division) calls on the Federal Government to introduce offering right of passage to*

persecuted European minorities of South Africa and Zimbabwe enabling them to re-settle in Australia.

As a consequence, Peter Dutton instructed the Home Affairs Department to consider bringing that severely persecuted white minority from South Africa to Australia on refugee visa grounds. Dutton called for them to be given special consideration, correctly reminding us that the group deserved our "special attention" due to the "horrific circumstances" they face at home.

To our utter disappointment no special visa was granted. As reported, the then Foreign Affairs Minister Julie Bishop refused to back Dutton and abide by the motion passed by the WA Liberal Party. While Bishop acknowledged this was a worthy response to an obvious humanitarian crisis with more than 19,000 murders, she said persecuted South Africans were not immediately eligible for humanitarian visas.[4] Needless to say, Scott Morrison remained entirely silent on the subject and refused to directly assist.

When Scott Morrison became Prime Minister, many expected a new kind of leadership in line with Christian values and principles – particularly after he explained to Australians the grief he felt and the tears he shed over the plight of genuine refugees. But when Asia Bibi was needing to escape from imminent death in November 2018, there was an opportunity for him to demonstrate his own integrity and the truthfulness of his own admissions.

Asia Bibi was a Christian farm labourer from Pakistan whose story began in June 2009 when she was picking berries with other farmworkers in a field in Punjab. She got into an argument with two Muslim women who refused to drink water she fetched because it had been touched by a Christian. Pakistan's blasphemy law carries the death sentence. Despite the harsh penalty, a remarkably light burden of proof needs to be produced and the accusers can refuse to repeat the allegation in court for fear of blaspheming themselves. As a result, Asia Bibi was convicted in 2010 on charges of blaspheming the prophet Muhammed.

Fortunately, the Pakistani Supreme Court overturned her conviction on grounds that there was no evidence to support condemnation. She was then acquitted after spending almost eight years on death row and solitary confinement. Because there were riots on the streets and radical Islamists vowed to assassinate her, Asia Bibi was forced to hide herself and apply for a refugee status in order to save her life.

On that occasion Dr Zimmermann publicly urged the Prime Minister on Sky News to show compassion and to offer political asylum to Asia Bibi, an innocent Christian woman who narrowly avoided the death penalty.[5] The case was a litmus test on whether Morrison really cared about the basic rights of an innocent person and fellow believer. All he actually needed to do was to grant her asylum.

To my utter dismay, in an abhorrently administrative letter the Australian government refused to offer such desperately needed assistance, citing her apparent failure to be granted U.N. Refugee Status and the pressures on the offshore component of its resettlement program.

Instead of offering asylum to a Christian woman in desperate need of assistance, the Morrison government argued that it would consider to offer asylum to Asia Bibi **only** if Canada or another country did not do so. The question is: *Why should Australia have to wait for a response from Canada first?* It's hard to see any justification for waiting on Canada. "Either it's the right thing to do or it isn't. And with extremists hunting her from house to house, it is important for us to act now", said Martyn Iles, Director of the Australian Christian Lobby (ACL).[6]

Unfortunately our "Christian" Prime Minister did not agree with him. What is significant is that the Morrison government gave over $47 million in aid to Pakistan that year. We should ask for our taxpayers' money back. President Trump was so angered by the behaviour of Pakistan's government over a range of issues that he had cut foreign aid to Pakistan, claiming the U.S. gets no co-operation in return. Remember how Osama bin Laden was found within five miles of a military academy while the whole civilised world was hunting for this arch-terrorist? And the Pakistani doctor who revealed his location to the US was sent to prison in Pakistan?

Naturally, the election of a Shorten-led Labor government in May 2019 would have been disastrous for the nation. The federal Labor Party apparently felt that talking about abortion on demand via "access to health services" would be electorally beneficial. In March 2019, Labor's spokesperson for women Tanya Plibersek announced a wide-ranging plan which included a move to use hospital funding agreements to "expect" states to provide abortion services in their public hospital systems.[7] As part of its strategy, Labor would review Medicare rebates around medical terminations (using the drug RU486) and help more GPs provide medical abortions.[8]

The Prime Minister claims to be a Christian so I presume he personally opposes abortion. And yet, he could not bring himself to say so. Sadly, when responding to Labor's abortion announcement, Morrison limited himself to state:

> This is a very controversial and sensitive issue and on these matters I have never sought to divide Australians on this. ... I don't find that debate one that tends to unite Australians and I certainly am not going to engage in the political elements of that discussion, because frankly I don't think it is good for our country.[9]

As can be seen, Morrison opposed Labor's abortion proposal on grounds that the issue apparently is too divisive. In his attempt to take the highest moral ground he ended up conveying the message that avoiding controversy is a higher good than stopping the killing of unborn children.

Another aspect of the Prime Minister's behaviour is his notorious disregard for freedom.

While Christian teaching emphasises that each person has worth and responsibility before God, our Prime Minister appears to believe that ultimate salvation can be achieved only via an all-powerful state. His first instincts are always authoritarian.

First of all, what has destroyed our economy is the behaviour of illiberal leaders such as Morrison himself. As so many others have pointed out since the pandemic began, there were far better and more efficient ways to fight this virus apart from draconian restrictions, bans and gross violations of the rule of law.[10] The Prime Minister appears to ignore that Australia is a country in which the federal government is derived from the law and not the law from the government.[11] The Morrison government has no more powers than those explicitly granted by the Australian Constitution.

We are supposedly living in a free and democratic society. It is quite extraordinary that a supposed democratic leader attempts to coerce citizens to do things they might not want to do. Instead of using the oppressive power of government to command his "subjects" to do whatever he might want, the Prime Minister should learn that true democratic leaders do not use their legal authority primarily but instead to persuade and convince their fellow citizens to do what is right.

Take also the Prime Minister's notorious disregard for freedom of speech. When Rugby Union player Israel Folau faced banishment for merely posting a "controversial" statement from the Bible on his Facebook page, Morrison's first reaction was to condemn him. "I thought they were terribly insensitive and obviously that is a matter for the ARU and they've taken that decision", he said of Folau's Facebook comments.[12]

Here you have a "Christian" Prime Minister literally throwing a fellow believer under the bus - joining the lynch mob against a brother in Christ who dares to exercise free speech by manifesting his opinion in the quoting of Scripture passages on a personal forum.

This was not the first time he had done such a thing. In April 2019, Victorian Liberals forced two Christian candidates to resign over so-called "homophobic" and "Islamophobic" comments. Peter Killin, Liberal candidate for Wills, was forced to resign after calling a certain Liberal MP a "notorious homosexual". Jeremy Hearn, Liberal candidate for Isaacs, was also forced to resign over comments about the threat of radical Islam that were made online.[13]

Instead of defending the right of Liberal candidates to express these opinions, speaking to journalists Morrison went on his way to warn the party to avoid such conservative candidates by "improving" its internal vetting procedures. "For the Liberal Party in this day and age when there is social media, multiple posting, that represents new challenges in the vetting of candidates" he said.[14]

Here you have a "Christian" politician who appears to have little regard for freedom of speech and freedom of religion. This could certainly lead one to seriously question the Christian maturity of anyone who supports the above actions. And what does it tell us about his commitment to basic human rights, if he cannot even take a strong stance for a fellow believer needing rescue from imminent death?

With friends like that, who needs enemies?

Chapter 1 endnotes

1   Based on A. Zimmermann, 'With Friends Like ScoMo, Who Needs Enemies?', *The Good Sauce*, July 8, 2021, at https://goodsauce.news/with-friends-like-scomo-who-needs-enemies/. Revised and updated by Prof Augusto Zimmermann and Dr Rocco Loiacono.

2   Nicola Berkovic, 'Coalition Worse than ALP on Human Rights', *The Australian*, February 6, 2020, at https://www.theaustralian.com.au/business/legal-affairs/coalition-worse-than-alp-on-human-rights/news-story/0bc3d71cd4daf8ab425f3bd5d8edba11.

3   Morgan Begg and Kristen Pereira, 'Legal Rights Audit 2019', Institute of Public Affairs, Melbourne/Vic, February 2020, p 1.

4   Olivia Caisley, 'South African Violence: Julie Bishop Refuses to Back Peter Dutton', *The Australian*, March 18, 2021, at https://www.theaustralian.com.au/nation/politics/south-africa-violence-julie-bishop-refuses-to-back-peter-dutton/news-story/dccf08470974bf1cccc3fbc020c32eed.

5   'Coalition Urged to Give Persecuted Pakistani Woman Asylum in Australia', *The Advertiser*, November 18, 2021, at https://www.adelaidenow.com.au/news/national/coalition-urged-to-give-persecuted-pakistani-woman-asylum-in-australia/video/3059e04b74d2ae7e13a2cdcc70f5110f.

6   Martyn Iles, 'Australia to Offer Asia Bibi Asylum', Australian Christian Lobby (ACL), November, 24, 2018, at https://www.acl.org.au/australia_to_offer_asia_bibi_asylum.

7   Judith Ireland, Labor pledges to tie hospital funding to abortion services', *The Sydney Morning Herald*, March 6, 2019, at https://www.smh.com.au/politics/federal/labor-pledges-to-tie-hospital-funding-to-abortion-services-20190305-p511uk.html.

8   Judith Ireland, 'It's About Women's Health: Inside Labor's Abortion Plan', *The Sydney Morning Herald*, March 10, 2021, at https://www.smh.com.au/politics/federal/it-s-about-women-s-health-inside-labor-s-abortion-plan-20190308-p512pf.html.

9   'Doorstop, Christmas Island – Transcript', Prime Minister of Australia, March 6, 2019, at https://www.pm.gov.au/media/doorstop-christmas-island.

10 See, for example, Augusto Zimmermann and Joshua Forrester (eds), *Fundamental rights in the Age of COVID-19*, Brisbane: Connor Court Publishing, 2021.

11 W. A. Wynes, *Legislative, Executive and Judicial Powers in Australia* (Sydney: The Law Book Co, 1955), vii.

12 Oliver Murray and Jai Bednall, 'Sports Reporter Says Rugby Australia Guilty of Homophobia', *News.Com.Au*, April 15, 2019, at https://www.news.com.au/sport/rugby/extremely-naive-or-stupid-israel-folau-lashed-on-offsiders/news-story/1ae58879db3a0a7abdefa003af9dee20.

13 Benjamin Preiss, 'Victorian Liberals' Horror Day on the Hustings', *The Age*, May 1, 2021, at https://amp.theage.com.au/federal-election-2019/that-notorious-homosexual-liberal-candidate-in-attack-on-tim-wilson-20190501-p51j0z.html.

14 Ibid.

The Morrison Government Is An Equal Opportunity Offender of Fundamental Rights[1]

Australians stuck overseas should not feel unwelcome to return home. Yet, in May 2021 when the travel ban on India was announced, any citizen flying back from that country faced punitive sanctions. The maximum penalties included a $66,000 fine or a five-year jail sentence.

It is the first time in Australian history that a government criminalises its citizens for attempting to return home. Yet, Prime Minister Scott Morrison refused to back down on the measure, arguing that it is necessary to use "emergency powers under the Biosecurity Act to protect Australia's health services and quarantine program."[2]

The prime minister has also dismissed accusations from Greens Party leader Adam Bandt that he is "racist" for imposing travel bans on those returning from India. Of course, such accusations are profoundly unfair because, when it comes to breaches of rights, the government is more of an "equal opportunity" provider.

Prior to the Covid-19 outbreak, the seminal Legal Rights Audit 2019 argued that 381 separate provisions had breached our fundamental rights via Acts of the Federal Parliament. "The Coalition government is trashing fundamental legal rights of all Australians, creating an unprecedented challenge to individual freedom and human dignity," says the main author, Institute of Public Affairs Research Fellow Morgan Begg.[3]

During the pandemic, the federal government restricted the right of citizens to leave the country without an exemption, of which few were granted. Although this is a nation of immigrants who have many friends and relatives overseas, including parents and children, the government oversaw a regime that has shut down international travel and enforces prohibitions that carry a whiff of authoritarianism. As a result, every Australian citizen needs to apply for special permission to visit parents or relatives overseas. They need special permission even to attend funerals or visit dying relatives.

However, this may be nothing compared to the situation of the 37,000 Australians still overseas (at the time of writing). Many experience trying conditions. Hundreds have posted Facebook messages to express the necessity of returning home, including to care for ill or dying relatives, because of losing their work or homes, or that the toll of being separated is "overwhelming".

"Essentially, you have a humanitarian disaster all around the world that Australian citizens are stranded in terrible conditions," argued Joseph Forgas AM, a psychology professor born in Hungary and migrated to Australia at 22 years of age as a refugee from communism.

Although he obtained special permission to attend his mother's funeral in Hungary, Forgas was unable to reunite with his wife and children in Australia. "My human rights are being violated. I am deeply disappointed, and I believe the Australian government has caused an immense damage to the country's reputation," he said.[4]

At the time of writing, there were an estimated 9,000 Australians in India, 600 of whom are classed as vulnerable. One Australian travelled to India to attend his father's funeral but is now concerned he will be separated indefinitely from his wife and two daughters who live in Adelaide. For such an individual travelling to mourn his own father's death, more compassion is needed.

A couple in their 70s were holidaying in the UK when the pandemic hit and have been trapped for almost a year without substantial assistance from authorities. There is also the PhD researcher who was unfortunate enough to attend a conference in Dublin, Ireland, in March 2020. She ended up having to stay for several months in the UK, with no job or stable accommodation. She sought help from the Australian High Commission in London, which told her to contact a local council about homeless accommodation.

Some Australian politicians have even raised the idea of stopping Australians from returning altogether. For example, During Western Australia's recent lockdown, State Premier Mark McGowan sought to attribute blame for the spread of the virus to individuals rather than scrutinise the faults of his state's quarantine system. Apparently, he is "furious" that some Australians still dare to travel overseas and blamed the federal government for allowing "too many Australians" to do so.[5]

International laws dictate a citizen's right to freedom of movement coupled with the right to return home. The latter is a principle most commonly invoked in refugee cases. Indeed, the International Covenant on Civil and Political Rights (ICCPR), to which Australia is a signatory, states that no one shall be "arbitrarily deprived of the right to enter his own country." For this reason, the UN Human Rights Committee, which oversees the implementation of the ICCPR, in May 2021 raised "serious concerns" about the Morrison government's decision to ban its own citizens from returning home.[6] Committee spokesperson Rupert Colville stated:

> *The UN Human Rights Commission … has emphasised the narrow authority to refuse nationals' return, and considers that there are few if any, circumstances in which deprivation of the right to enter one's own country could be reasonable.*

Amid these travel bans, it does appear that, after all, some people are actually "more equal than others." It is a two-tiered system where the more powerful and famous can receive special treatment compared to ordinary people. For example, in the same week the government began halving arrival caps for Australians, citing the threat posed by the UK variant of Covid-19, it allowed more than 1,700 tennis players, their staff and others to enter the country for the Australian Open tennis tournament.

The prime minister contends that the cap to Australians returning home must continue because the quarantine systems cannot handle the influx of arrivals. However, Hollywood seems to have been exempt.[7] As reported, "It began with Zac Efron. Then Mark Wahlberg flew over, Matt Damon jetted in, and a dozen other celebrities followed, all to set up temporary homes in Australia."[8] These celebrities can come and freely enjoy our beaches, bars, and nightclubs, particularly in Sydney. Meanwhile, at least 37,000 Australians are trapped overseas, desperately waiting to return home.

The Prime Minister needs more political will and compassion to help Australian citizens. When it comes to breaches of fundamental rights, the Morrison government is not "racist" but rather an "equal opportunity" provider!

Chapter 2 endnotes

1   Based on: A. Zimmermann, 'The Australian Government is an "Equal Opportunity"
     Offender of Civilian Rights', *The Epoch Times*, May 6, 2021, at https://www.
     theepochtimes.com/the-australian-government-is-an-equal-opportunity-offender-of-
     civilian-rights_3804852.html. Revised and updated by Prof Augusto Zimmermann
     and Dr Rocco Loiacono.

2   Jade Gailberger and Finn McHugh, 'Aussies Returning from India Face Jail, Fines', *The
     Australian*, May 3, 2021, at https://www.theaustralian.com.au/breaking-news/aussies-
     returning-from-india-face-jail-fines/news-story/75cc0400320371a93515405473fbd5
     8b.

3   Morgan Begg and Kristen Pereira, 'Legal Rights Audit 2019', Institute of Public Affairs,
     Melbourne/Vic, February 2020, p 1.

4   'Politicians Again Turn Coronavirus Problem Into A Human Disaster', *Sky News*,
     September 15, 2020, at https://www.skynews.com.au/details/_6190888629001.

5   Naaman Zhou, 'WA premier furious that residents are travelling overseas as Covid
     lockdown continues', *The Guardian Australia*, April 25, 2021, at https://www.
     theguardian.com/australia-news/2021/apr/25/western-australia-reports-no-new-
     cases-of-locally-acquired-covid-on-day-two-of-lockdown.

6   Jorge Branco, 'UN Human Rights Committee Raises Serious Concerns Over India
     Travel Ban', 9News, May 5, 2021, at https://www.9news.com.au/national/coronavirus-
     india-travel-ban-pressure-mounts-un-human-rights-committee/944c25b9-6ba1-
     4390-89fb-ab57f7386a08.

7   Sophie Williams, 'Tennis stars' arrival angers stranded Australians', *BBC News*, January
     16, 2021, at https://www.bbc.com/news/world-australia-55683035.

8   Frances Mao, 'Celebrities in Australia Anger Stranded Citizens Over Double Standard',
     BBC News, April 1, 2021, at https://www.bbc.com/news/world-australia-55851074.

Chapter 3

ScoMo's Had Enough – No More Free Speech[1]

Those terrible shootings in the mosque in New Zealand in May 2019 can never be justified. It was pure evil and the Australian man who committed such an appalling act deserves to receive, at the very least, life imprisonment.

Within minutes of that terrible tragedy, Scott Morrison made a public statement, asserting that this man massacred worshippers in an act of "an extremist right-wing violent terrorism". This is what the Prime Minister posted on his Twitter account on March 15, 2019: "I condemn the violent, extremist, right-wing terrorist attack that has stolen the lives of so many innocent New Zealanders".[2]

The words employed by the Prime Minister were deeply troubling as they could incite violence or at least great animosity against so-called "right wingers". He simply assumed the terrorist was "right-wing" prior to any assessment of the facts. As it turns out, the terrorist who killed 50 Muslims at the mosque in New Zealand is not a right-winger. Instead, he is a self-described "anarchist" and a "radical environmentalist". In his mind the world is dying from over-population, but over-population of the "wrong" kind.

In his own "manifesto", he described himself as an "eco-fascist" and an admirer of Communist China. How can any person, in addition to expressing his admiration for Communist China, and who has described himself as an "eco-fascist" and wants "no part of" conservatism, possibly be described as a *"right winger"*?[3]

Answering a question in his manifesto "Are you a conservative?", the gunman stated: "No, conservatism is corporatism in disguise, I want no part of it." "Conservatism is dead, thank god," he wrote.

The gunman also expressed his admiration for Communist China. "The nation with the closest political and social values to my own is the People's Republic of China," he wrote.[4] He also disavowed President Trump from the standpoint of his conservative policies and decisions. In answer to the question: "Were you a supporter of Donald Trump?", he replied: "Dear god, of course I am not."

And before one claims that we have not been accurate because the gunman also described himself as an eco-fascist, perhaps a few words may help understand what fascism actually means and where it can actually be placed in the ideological spectrum.

Fascism was first established in Italy after the World War I. Its creator, Benito Mussolini, was the son of an anarchist father and a Marxist mother. In 1912, he became "one of the most effective and widely read socialist journalists in Europe". In that year Mussolini was appointed the head of the Socialist Party opposing "bourgeois" parliaments and proposing that Italian socialism should be thoroughly Marxist.

"Marx", wrote Mussolini, "is the father and teacher ... he is the magnificent philosopher of working-class violence". On the eve of World War II, he predicted: "With the unleashing of a mighty clash of peoples, the bourgeoisie is playing its last card and calls forth on the world scene that which Karl Marx called the sixth great power: the socialist revolution".[5]

The French historian François Furet explains that "Communism and Fascism grew up on the same soil, the soil of Italian Socialism". According to Furet, "Mussolini was a member of the revolutionary wing of the Socialist movement prior to supporting Italy's entry into the war; then, immediately afterward, he found himself in violent conflict with the Bolshevik-leaning leaders of his former party".[6]

Above all, Mussolini agreed with Lenin, the Founder and leader of the Soviet Union, that violence was a useful and ultimately necessary means to achieve complete social dominance and full political power.

This should dissipate once and for all the false assumption that fascism is a right-wing ideology. It is certainly not.

Above all, the gunman is definitely not a right-wing extremist as falsely stated by our Prime Minister. Instead, the murderer is an extremist who absolutely hates capitalism, free markets, and free trade but he loves the Communist Chinese government and fascism, which is actually a form of nationalist socialism.

In sum, the gunman is a radical environmentalist and sympathiser of communist regimes, who openly despises mainstream conservatism. Hence his strong condemnation for mainstream conservatives, whom he dismissed as "milquetoast civic nationalist boomers".

So why would the Prime Minister choose to blame "right-wing extremism" rather than left-wing extremism? It could be that Morrison actually subscribes to the leftist narrative, which seeks every opportunity to undermine conservatives and link us to violence. It is as if this incident has caused him to nail his colours to the mast.

It seems that when push comes to shove that Morrison will side with the Left every time. Surely, it is certainly incongruous for him to lead what is supposed to be a right-wing government but falsely associate his own government to a murderer by calling him a "right winger".

Chapter 3 endnotes

1   Based on the article: A Zimmermann, 'ScoMo's Had Enough – No More Free Speech', *The Unschakled*, March 20, 2019, at https://www.theunshackled.net/rundown/ scomos-had-enough-no-more-free-speech/ Revised and updated by Prof Augusto Zimmermann and Dr Rocco Loiacono.

2   Twitter, Scott Morrison, March 15, 2019, at https://twitter.com/scottmorrisonmp/ status/1106437117960323072?lang=en.

3   Rod Dreher, 'Radicalization & Degeneration', *The American Conservative*, March 15, 2019, at https://www.theamericanconservative.com/dreher/radicalization-degeneration-brenton-tarrant-white-supremacist/.

4   Isabella Steger and Echo Huang, 'The New Zealand Shooter Finds Support in Islamophobic Corners of China's Internet', *Quartz*, March 26, 2019, at https:// qz.com/1575028/new-zealand-shooter-finds-fans-in-islamophobic-corners-of-chinas-internet/.

5   Quoted in Paul Johnson, *Modern Times: The World From The Twenties to the Nineties* (New York/NY: Harper Perennial, 2001), p 57.

6   François Furet, *The Passing of an Illusion: The Idea of Communism in the Twentieth Century* (University of Chicago Press, 1999), p 22.

Where's the Prime Minister on the Free Speech Crisis?[1]

GoFundMe's shutdown in June 2019 of Israel Folau's fundraising page for "violation of … terms of service" was a troubling development for religious freedom and has disturbing implications for freedom of speech. GoFundMe has basically declared Folau *persona non grata* due to his religious convictions and the right to express such convictions.

As correctly noted by the *Human Rights Law Alliance* managing director, John Steenhof, in the Nine Newspapers, "GoFundMe's conduct should alarm all Australians interested in fair and equal access to justice. Anyone who wants to fundraise to have their day in an Australian court now has an extra barrier".[2]

Apparently, however, the Prime Minister still does not fully appreciate the fight we are in. When asked about the closure of Mr Folau's fundraiser, Scott Morrison said: "I think that the issue has had enough oxygen."

By contrast, NSW Legislative Council member Mark Latham, who defended Mr Folau in his maiden speech to parliament earlier in 2019, said *GoFundMe's* decision was "excessive use of corporate power". He tweeted: "Lefties scoffed when I said the absence of religious freedom protections would lead to a reign of terror against Christians. In all aspects of the Folau matter, it's easy to see what's happening."

This is a rather interesting situation. The agnostic Latham defends freedom of religion and freedom of speech for Christians, but the "Christian PM" cowardly refuses to make a comment. He even stated that Folau's comments were unacceptable. "I thought they were terribly insensitive and obviously that is a matter for the ARU and they've taken that decision," Morrison said.

Here you have a "Christian" Prime Minister who appears to have no regard for freedom of speech and freedom of religion. He is literally throwing a fellow believer under the bus – joining the lynch mob against a brother in Christ who simply dared to exercise his freedom of religion by freely manifesting his opinion.

Folau was simply quoting the Bible. What is next? The Bible banned in Australia?

After all, *GoFundMe* has shut down the fundraiser of a religious person who has been punished for simply expressing a mainstream Christian viewpoint, a fundraiser supported by thousands of Australians. They were charged a fee to use this disconnected service. And yet, as correctly stated by Christian activist and social commentator Bernard Gaynor,

> It is illegal to discriminate in the terms on which goods or services are supplied… And, just to make it clear, it is even prohibited to treat another person unfavourably in any way in connection with the supply of goods or services.[3]

Our Prime Minister not only needs to know better what the law says, but also to realise that he has been returned to office not because he has done anything particularly good for our country.

On the contrary, he is still a Prime Minister only because the opposition leader was truly appalling and not a feasible option. Indeed, Bill Shorten is an old-fashioned socialist who has absolutely no regard for individual rights and freedoms. This is why, and only why, Australian citizens decided to return the Coalition to power. It was the best of two rather undesirable options.

Curiously, the Prime Minister has a long track record of disregard for freedom of speech. About five years ago he fiercely resisted any debate over free speech and section 18C of the *Racial Discrimination Act*, contending that changing that notorious provision 'would not help reduce unemployment or improve any other economic metric'. His argument was rather disquieting:

> I know there are lot of people who are interested in this issue. As a senior figure in this government … I know this issue doesn't create one job, doesn't open one business, doesn't give anyone one extra hour … I don't see any intersection between that issue and those priorities.[4]

In an interview with the then Fairfax Media, in December 2017, the now Prime Minister expressed his support for further restrictions to free speech on religious grounds. Morrison commented:

> It all starts when you allow … mockery to be made of your faith or your religious festivals — it always starts innocently and it's always said it is just a joke — just like most discrimination does. And I'm just gonna call that out … I've just taken the decision more recently, I'm just not going to put up with that any more, I don't think my colleagues are either. Where I think people are being offensive to religion in this country — whichever religion that might be … well, we will just call it out and we will demand the … respect that people should provide to all religions.[5]

One should remind the Prime Minister that, in a pluralistic society, people of different faiths and of no faith should avoid being "uncomfortable" in robust conversations about religion.

Further, it is simply not acceptable in a true democracy to protect any religious group from being "offended" without grievously infringing on the constitutionally implied freedom of political communication of others who strongly disagree with them. The last thing we need in this country is for a Commonwealth parliament to introduce any further anti-discrimination laws based on religious grounds.

Chapter 4 endnotes

1   Based on the article: A Zimmermann, 'Where's the Prime Minister on the Free Speech Crisis?', *The Spectator Australia*, June 26, 2019, at https://www.spectator.com.au/2019/06/wheres-the-prime-minister-on-the-free-speech-crisis/. Revised and updated by Prof Augusto Zimmermann and Dr Rocco Loiacono.

2   John Steenhof, 'GoFundMe Has Set Itself Up as Judge, Jury and Executioner', *Sydney Morning Herald*, June 24, 2019, at https://www.smh.com.au/sport/rugby-union/gofundme-has-set-itself-up-as-judge-jury-and-executioner-20190624-p520pe.html.

3   Bernard Gaynor, 'GoFundMe breaks the law', June 24, 2019, at https://www.bernardgaynor.com.au/2019/06/24/gofundme-breaks-the-law/.

4   Michael Koziol, 'Scott Morrison Warns Against Internal Fight Over Free Speech Laws: 'It Does Not Create One Job'', *The Sydney Morning Herald*, March 1, 2017, at https://www.smh.com.au/politics/federal/fundamental-breach-of-faith-george-christensen-berates-boss-barnaby-joyce-over-race-hate-laws-20170302-guovfg.html.

5   James Massola, "I'm Not Going To Put Up With It Any More': Morrison Vows to Defend Christianity in 2018', *The Canberra Times*, December 21, 2017, at https://www.canberratimes.com.au/story/6024582/im-not-going-to-put-up-with-it-any-more-morrison-vows-to-defend-christianity-in-2018/.

Chapter 5

The Jaundiced Pursuit of Agents of Foreign Influence[1]

The Morrison Government promised that the *Foreign Influence Transparency Scheme Act 2018* (FITS) would expose dangerous foreign influences well-known to our security agencies. In 2018, the then Attorney-General Christian Porter stated that this new legislation would "safeguard the nation's democracy". "FITS will provide visibility of the forms and sources of foreign influence in Australia's governmental and political processes,"[2] he said.

As can be seen, this law was supposed to protect us from foreign undemocratic regimes attempting to influence our citizens. However, when a conservative group held a conference to discuss individual rights and freedoms in conjunction with a group from our greatest ally, the United States, eight senior bureaucrats working at the Attorney-General's Department decided to use the poorly drafted legislation against the person who co-hosted this conference. Apparently these bureaucrats believe that a conference about fundamental rights poses a great threat to Australia!

Former Prime Minister Tony Abbott became one of the first individuals targeted under the legislation. He was requested to register as an "agent of foreign influence" under such national security laws, for simply addressing the *Conservative Political Action Conference* (CPAC) in August 2019. Mr Abbott has served the country's best interests over his entire working career but was being hounded by faceless bureaucrats in Canberra, and all courtesy of the Morrison government.

Andrew Cooper, the event's main organiser, was also requested to register as an agent of foreign influence under such legislation. He is the founder of *Liberty Works*, "an Australian based not-for-profit organisation that advocates for a drastic reduction in government control over people's economic and personal lives. [They] celebrate liberty where it exists and fight the erosion of liberty when it's under threat."

It looks like a desperately needed organisation, and certainly not a threat to our national security, but rather to the security of governments with authoritarian inclinations. However, because Liberty Works has co-hosted a CPAC conference with the American Conservative Union (ACU), Mr Cooper was ordered by the Attorney-General's Department to hand over documents and threatened with imprisonment if he failed to do so.

CPAC is hosted by the ACU and it can be described as a Centre-Right annual conference attended by conservative and libertarian activists and elected officials from across the United States and beyond. It has been a significant annual event since 1974, when the first CPAC was held with Ronald Reagan as the inaugural keynote speaker.

Australia's first CPAC was held in August 2019, with guest speakers including Tony Abbott, Brexit campaign leader Nigel Farage, former *Breitbart* editor-in-chief Raheem Kassam, Liberal Senator Amanda Stoker, and New South Wales One Nation leader Mark Latham.

Despite these mainstream speakers, Labor's home affairs spokeswoman, Kristina Keneally, warned of an "alt-right takeover" and "rising white supremacism" in Australia. It was clearly a ridiculous statement, although typical of left-wing politicians who have no regard for free speech and are completely intolerant of people upholding conservative views.

Bizarrely, official letters were sent to Cooper and Abbott within days of Keneally's demented comment, making it hard for the Attorney-General's Department to dissociate itself from such a display of leftist bias. Indeed, Ms Keneally herself has stated that the FITS laws have been properly implemented and precisely as the government had intended.

The letter from the Attorney-General's Department to Mr Cooper was sent by Sarah Chidgey, the deputy secretary of the Integrity and International Group. It advised him to provide all documents "detailing any understandings or arrangement between Liberty Works and ACU".[3] "This is government overreach worthy of the Chinese Communist Party in Hong Kong," Cooper said.

Speaking of the Chinese government, one should be reminded of recent initiatives undertaken by the Premier of Victoria, Daniel Andrews, at the Belt and Road Forum in Beijing in May 2019. Reportedly Andrews, after his attendance at the forum, was touting his state's memorandum of understanding with the Chinese government as an opportunity for "more trade and more Victorian jobs and an even stronger relationship with China". Andrews reportedly stated: "Victoria is proud of its longstanding and valued partnership with China and this new Framework Agreement helps take it to the next level. We don't see China as our good customers, we see them as our good friends."

A quiet investigation of Labor politicians' relations with China and various Islamic regimes, state and non-state, is therefore required. Ms Chidgey and her colleagues in the Attorney-General's Department do not stand for election; they use more undemocratic ways to impose their leftist interpretation of the law.

But these bureaucrats should not take all the blame. How can such a law possibly allow this kind of draconian overreach?

According to Janet Albrechtsen, this mess started with a Coalition government that concocted, drafted and enacted laws "riddled with uncertainty about who must register, who is a foreign government, the meaning of an 'arrangement', and the intended scope of the nexus between a foreign principal and the person acting on their behalf are too vague, and hence potentially far-reaching".[4]

When a law can so arbitrarily be used to target even a former prime minister for daring to speak at a conservative conference that includes foreigners, it is not so hard to imagine that this is a bad law that can be easily used by overzealous bureaucrats in pursuit of everyone who dares to engage in such political conversations. This is obviously a violation of our constitutionally implied freedom of political communication. According to Anne Twomey, an author and constitutional law professor at the University of Sydney Law School, the enforcement of such legislation "could force thousands of people, including authors, academics and publishers, to register as agents of other countries".

This is lawfare of the worst kind, and the process is the punishment. But it is not the bureaucrats responsible for the application of laws, but rather the elected government that introduced and passed them, which bears the primary responsibility for the problem. The Morrison government needs to admit its shortcomings. Such a "conservative" government should assume that poorly drafted laws could be easily weaponised by hostile civil servants, who are simply using the tools the government of the day has made available to them against their preferred political targets. As Albrechtsen points out:

> [T]he upshot is that a Liberal-led government enacted laws that can be used to deliver patently illiberal outcomes. It has invited the likes of Kristina Keneally to say, with all the seriousness of a clown, that these laws are working just fine. Even worse, if that is possible, precedents such as these ensure that Labor will have a field day eroding freedoms when it is next in government.[5]

An internal document from the Attorney-General's Department, obtained by the Institute of Public Affairs, reveals that Labor's legal affairs spokesman, Mark Dreyfus, "specifically raised the upcoming Conservative Political Action Conference (CPAC) to be held in Sydney on 9-11 August 2019, as an example of an event that may trigger registration obligations under the scheme and asked what the department planned to do about it".

Following Dreyfus's intervention, the Attorney-General's Department wrote to Mr Cooper, requiring him to register. He became the first person under the scheme to be ordered to hand over documents and threatened with imprisonment if he failed to do so.

Mr Cooper is not mistaken to consider that "Mr Dreyfus has deliberately and methodically sought to use the state to censor the free speech of his political opponents. It is a cowardly act." Indeed, the shadow attorney-general is a serial offender when it comes to referring his political enemies for investigation. He knows full well the reason this legislation was endorsed by Parliament following the revelations of Chinese influence in the Dastyari affair and yet chose to use it to attack his political opponents. His mindset is hardly one that we should expect of the alternative attorney-general.

It appears therefore that Labor and left-wing bureaucrats are colluding and using the legislation as an instrument of political persecution against conservatives and libertarians. However, the Morrison government was the enabler of these illiberal actions by the bureaucrats working at the Attorney-General's Department.

These laws enacted by the Morrison government are "fit for purpose" only in a totalitarian regime, not a liberal democracy. They would not be surprising under a leftist party of illiberal inclinations such as Labor, but it is a great disappointment to see a "Liberal" government implement draconian laws that potentially interfere with everyone and everything.

This episode also shows that the Morrison government has lost control over its bureaucracy, which is supposed to serve them and implement their policies. These unelected bureaucrats seem to have effective control over government policy, like the Stasi of East Germany or the KGB in the Soviet Union. As Abbott said when he received his letter on August 8, 2019: "It's oppressive, it's coercive. I thought the commissars had gone when the bloody Soviet Union went out of business." And Cooper has also rightfully stated that this government overreach makes him feel very much as if "the Stasi is holding me in 1950s East Berlin and I am being threatened with jail because I cannot provide them with information that I do not have".

One problem is that the legislation was enacted to deter influence from Communist China but without naming the country. The law has never been applied against Chinese influence and there has actually been a dramatic rise in Chinese propaganda emanating from "Confucius Centres" at Australian schools and universities.

Why has the Department not sent a Section 45(2) notice to Australian universities that have such centres to explain why their institution is being influenced by a foreign entity, namely the Chinese Communist government? According to Michael Rubin, a resident scholar at the American Enterprise Institute and a frequent visitor to Australia:

> *Beijing launders donations through a network of Confucius Institutes to about a dozen Australian universities … These Chinese studies institutes may teach language but they have become centres for Chinese government intelligence and control, including monitoring and censorship of those who stray off the academic paths with which Beijing is comfortable.*[6]

The situation becomes even more bizarre when Australian universities also have centres which are financially sponsored by Islamic regimes of the Middle East. For instance, the University of Western Australia holds the notorious "Centre for Muslim States and Societies" and the Australian National University's "Centre for Arab and Islamic Studies" openly receives money donated by the

United Arab Emirates, Qatar, Turkey and Iran directly or indirectly. As for the sort of "academic work" this Islamic centre provides, a whitewash of the terrorist group Hamas and its genocidal charter has been a standard practice there.

Just six years ago, the ANU centre for Islamic Studies proudly hosted a 9/11 conspiracy theorist who dismissed concerns about Ayatollah Khomeini's summary executions, repression of women and general human rights abuses as "happily false". Apparently, the university even changed the name of that centre from "Middle East and Central Asian Studies" to "Arab and Islamic Studies" after a large Emirati donation, thus accepting foreign money and influence that undermines standards of academic integrity, autonomy and freedom.

In a June 2018 article in *The Australian*, the Australian Jewish Association president, Dr David Adler, argued that the ANU's acceptance of foreign funding for a Centre for Arab and Islamic Studies is inconsistent with its reasoning for abandoning plans for a course in Western civilisation. His views "echoed the sentiments of various politicians who have accused the university of double standards following the revelation that its Centre for Arab and Islamic Studies had accepted millions of dollars in donations from the United Arab Emirates and the Iranian and Turkish governments". Dr Adler stated:

> *We have seen Islamic countries invest in university education around the world very substantially and we know that ANU has a program of Arabic and Islamic studies and received millions in funding from Arab and Islamic countries. There is a fundamental question that needs to be answered here: why can ANU resolve their issues of academic autonomy in some areas of study but not when it comes to Western civilisation?*[7]

Apparently, the faceless bureaucrats in the Attorney-General's Department see no problem with Australian universities receiving foreign money and influence from communist and Islamic regimes.[8] By targeting only conservatives and libertarians, these bureaucrats have shown their leftist bias and have used a bad law for their own political interest. However, the Morrison government appears to have no control over its own departments.

Did the then Attorney-General punish the bureaucrats responsible for such an appalling overreach? It seems Christian Porter stated that the staff overseeing the scheme would be moved, which is totally inadequate. Public servants act on their minister's authorisation, so there was no excuse for the Morrison government not to act more firmly.

However, this government seems unable or unwilling to confront them and get them under control. The exercise of public discretion is conditional on the application of reasonableness and common sense. In a democracy, public servants cannot act arbitrarily, picking and choosing their own targets. The Attorney-General is the Crown official responsible for overseeing these processes, and he should know it. If he lacks the courage to stand up to public servants who act arbitrarily, he should step down or be forced to resign.

Giving unelected public servants so much autonomy is a recipe for disaster. Besides, nearly every legislation has a provision allowing for ministerial intervention when processes go off the rails. If this Act does not contain a section allowing for ministerial intervention, then it is poorly drafted and an open invitation to arbitrariness.

The Institute of Public Affairs lodged a Freedom of Information request, asking for documents and correspondence between senior executive-level public servants between March and November that mention Cooper, Abbott, CPAC and ACU. More than 1,300 documents relating to these names were captured from eight full-time public servants in a seven-month period, which "suggests a co-ordinated surveillance operation being run by unelected and unaccountable bureaucrats under the Attorney-General's nose".[9]

According to Evan Mulholland, Director of Communications at the Institute of Public Affairs, "given the extent of Chinese influence reported in the media … it is unacceptable that Australian public servants in the Attorney-General's Department have devoted such a significant amount of time and resources to targeting Australians because of their political beliefs". Evidently if you are a "right-winger" and an advocate for individual rights and freedoms, you are now deemed to be up there with the Islamic State. We doubt any of the imams who hold conferences advocating violence against non-believers have been called to account under this legislation.

Let us be absolutely clear. This legislation can be (and has been) easily used by the government to attack conservative Australians. It is almost unbelievable that a so-called "Liberal" government would viciously attack free speech in this country. But, then again, we're talking about a government that has not amended or repealed the notorious section 18C of the *Racial Discrimination Act*.

There is little doubt that the low threshold set in section 18C by the inclusion of the words "offend, insult, humiliate" raises real questions as to whether such provision would be supported by the Constitution. The external affairs power appears to be the head of federal legislative power. However, legislation relying on this head of power must be capable of being reasonably "appropriate and adapted" to treaty obligations, which is definitely not the case. Section 18C goes considerably further than the obligations imposed on Australia to guard against racial hatred under international law.

If this wasn't enough, section 18C also infringes the implied freedom of communication concerning political and governmental matters. Under the Constitution, our citizens must be able to discuss political matters, including those involving race, colour, ethnicity and nationality. Australians are a sovereign people and such communication is critical to democratic law-making, and to holding both the executive and the legislature branches of government accountable to the Australian people. In *Attorney-General (SA) v Corporation of the City of Adelaide* (2013), Chief Justice Robert French stated:

> *Freedom of speech is a long-established common law freedom ... linked to the proper functioning of representative democracies and on that basis has informed the application of public interest considerations to claimed restraints upon publication of information.*[10]

These bad laws are having a detrimental impact on freedom of speech without having a corresponding positive impact in eliminating racial discrimination. For instance, university students in Queensland, after raising an issue of racial discrimination involving their eviction from a computer lab which was reserved for one particular ethnic group at the expense of all other ethnic groups, were themselves accused of racial discrimination under section 18C.

Clearly, freedom of speech remains under serious threat in Australia, despite several years of Coalition government. The Morrison government should have long ago undertaken a comprehensive review of all anti-free-speech legislation, including section 18C. It should propose legislation that eliminates excesses and streamlines processes, while retaining the ability of our security services to do their job.

Furthermore, it is important to remind our Liberal members of parliament that the task of government in solving problems is not achieved by introducing more bad legislation. The Morrison government has the moral duty not only to repeal this terrible piece of legislation, but also all the numerous other bad laws that continue to undermine free speech, including FITS. As Albrechtsen notes, "the evil nature of totalitarianism is not what happens outside the law. It happens when the law, or a veneer of legality, is used, often in the name of national security, to control what good people do, be it sharing ideas or speaking out against tyranny."[11]

It is time for the Prime Minister to come out of his comfort zone. Official apologies should have been issued to Mr Cooper and Mr Abbott, and a comprehensive review begun of the *Foreign Influence Transparency Scheme Act*. Continuing inaction only indicates that this government is comfortable with the appalling situation and the damage being done to Australia's democracy.

Above all, the improper understanding of the role of government in a free society is one of the reasons we need more organisations like CPAC, to hold government accountable and give citizens a voice. What we badly need in this country is a government that truly values fundamental rights and freedoms. The government of Scott Morrison is failing us miserably in this regard. It is time for people who truly believe in the basic rights of the individual over the state to stand up against an increasingly oppressive Australian government.

Chapter 5 endnotes

1   Based on: A. Zimmermann, 'The Jaundiced Pursuit of Agents of Foreign Influence', *Quadrant Magazine*, Vol. LXIV, No.5, May 2020, pp 42-45. Revised and updated by Prof Augusto Zimmermann and Dr Rocco Loiacono.

2   See generally: Foreign Influence Transparency Scheme Legislation Amendment Bill 2018 at https://www.aph.gov.au/About_Parliament/Parliamentary_Departments/ Parliamentary_Library/FlagPost/2018/December/Foreign_Influence_ Transparency_Scheme_Legislation_Amendment_Bill_2018.

3   Janet Albrechtsen and Joe Kelly, 'Tony Abbot Declares: I'm not an Agent of Foreign Influence', *The Australian*, November 2, 2019, at https://www.theaustralian.com.au/ nation/politics/tony-abbott-declares-im-not-an-agent-of-foreign-influence/news-story/da7994187fc74acd6797c3d5918b77a0.

4   Ibid.

5   Janet Albrechtsen, 'Would Sir Humphrey Appleby Approve? No, Minister', *The Australian*, November 6, 2019, at https://www.theaustralian.com.au/ commentary/would-sir-humphrey-appleby-approve-no-minister/news-story/ e04476f7108024ac1863d8e52588ce3b.

6   Michael Rubin, 'Islamic Centre Mocks ANU Claim To Academic Independence', *The Australian*, June 14, 2018, at https://www.theaustralian.com.au/opinion/islamic-centre-mocks-anu-claim-to-academic-authority/news-story/648bea3cd6ce0849615d 5cf015c3c7da.

7   Rebecca Urban, 'ANU Has Been Islamised, Claims Jewish Lobby Group', *The Australian*, June 12, 2018, at https://www.theaustralian.com.au/higher-education/anu-has-been-islamised-claims-jewish-lobby-group/news-story/e880a9050ab005df6f d1191bff10dd61.

8   See: https://chinamatters.org.au/wp-content/uploads/2019/10/18102019-Eighth-National-Meeting-of-China-Matters-participant-list-.pdf.

9   Evan Mulholland, 'There May Be 1300 Reasons This Law Does Not Work', *The Australian*, November 29, 2019, at https://ipa.org.au/ipa-today/there-may-be-1300-reasons-this-law-does-not-work.

10 *Attorney-General (SA) v Corporation of the City of Adelaide* [2013] HCA 3, 43.

11 Janet Albrechtsen, 'Shades of Stasiland in Attorney-General's Office', *The Australian*, November 2, 2019, at https://www.theaustralian.com.au/inquirer/shades-of-stasiland-in-attorneygenerals-office/news-story/d744396439cba6ca1862fac02eedef3b.

Chapter 6

Morrison Urges Social Media Bosses to Practice More Censorship[1]

On 8th January 2021, Twitter, a social network, announced that it was "permanently suspending" U.S. President Donald Trump's account. Other social networks took a similarly tough line. For example, Facebook said that President Trump's account would be banned for "at least" the remainder of his term in office, which was due to expire on January 20, 2021.

We should not be surprised. Politicians such as the Australian Prime Minister have constantly demanded more social media censorship of so-called "right-wing extremism". In March 2019, in a letter to the Chair of the G-20 Summit in Osaka, Japanese Prime Minister Shinzo Abe, Mr Morrison argued that social media managers should face jail unless they co-operated with stopping their platforms being used to spread "right-wing extremism".

Also in March 2019, in an interview on the Seven Network Sunrise program, the Prime Minister stated: "If they can write an algorithm to make sure that the ADs they want you to see can appear on your mobile phone, then I'm quite confident they can write an algorithm to screen out hate content on social media platforms".[2]

Morrison's claims are not just absurd. They constitute an egregious form of undemocratic censorship.

Toby Walsh is professor of artificial intelligence at the University of NSW. He explains that the comparison is inappropriate because advertising is quite imprecise. "Filtering social media is something you want to do with much greater accuracy", Professor Walsh said.[3]

Professor Jean Burgess is director of the QUT's Digital Media Research Centre. She says algorithms "have pretty big limitations", and noted that "tacking hate speech also comes with … complexities that machine learning is not yet particularly good at dealing with".

Of course, social media platforms such as YouTube and Facebook are already using algorithms to detect alleged "hate content" which is then reviewed by employees of these organisations. On 26 March 2019, however, the Prime Minister summoned the representatives of these social media companies (including Google, Facebook, and Twitter) to a meeting in Brisbane. There he outlined a series of draconian measures aimed at forcing them to rapidly remove whatever the government deems to be "abhorrent material". "We are considering all options to keep Australians safe", Morrison said.[4]

By inciting the regulation of speech by social media, the Prime Minister provoked serious censorship in the process. His statements were followed by the social media's censorship of dissenting opinions. YouTube now employs more than 10,000 reviewers for this, while Facebook employs at least 15,000.

In addition, the Morrison government has passed legislation that could see social media executives in jail and companies fined for failing to take down "abhorrent material expeditiously". Under this legislation, anyone found guilty of using an online service to "cause offence" could be jailed for up to five years.[5]

These measures are a part of international efforts to suppress freedom of speech online. However, Labor and the Greens enthusiastically backed this egregious assault on democratic rights. Indeed, all the major political parties have proposed measures to stop so-called "hate speech" from being posted on social media outlets.

Of course, much speech that is criticised as "hate speech" is no more than a proper response to speech by the culturally privileged groups. They have a particular desire to suppress any form of speech that might constitute a threat to their hegemonic discourse.

Morrison has even floated the possibility of a ban on all social media live streaming, which would prevent ordinary people from broadcasting significant social and political events and airing their views to a live audience online. Arguably, live streaming has been used in Australia and internationally to document police arbitrariness and government attacks on pro-freedom protesters and to broadcast popular demonstrations against draconian measures to a global audience.

It goes without saying that if the Prime Minister and other politicians consider themselves superior to everybody else (as being by the nature of their position supposedly better than others), it follows that it automatically becomes "hateful" to criticise them on social media more robustly. If we lived in a real democracy then no Australian government would prevent us from freely addressing political and governmental matters, even when such discussion involves issues that are regarded as "controversial" in the eyes of a small minority of privileged individuals.

Above all, there is one important lesson to be learned from such a drive to instigate all this social media censorship and other authoritarian measures: it undeniably reveals the profound contempt held by the country's ruling elites for the average Australian citizen.

Chapter 6 endnotes

1   Based on: A. Zimmermann, 'Morrison Urges Social Media Bosses to Practice More Censorship', *Caldron Pool*, January 15, 2021, at https://caldronpool.com/morrison-urges-social-media-bosses-to-practice-more-censorship/. Revised and updated by Prof Augusto Zimmermann and Dr Rocco Loiacono.

2   Eliza Laschon and Setphanie Dalzell, 'Scott Morrison Wants Crackdown On Social Media Companies After Sharing of Christchurch Shootings Footage', ABCNews, March 19, 2019, at https://www.abc.net.au/news/2019-03-19/scott-morrison-social-media-companies-christchurch-shootings/10915246.

3   Fact Check, 'Scott Morrison Said Hate Content on Social Media Could be Automatically Screened Out by Algorithms', ABC News, April 18, 2019, at https://www.abc.net.au/news/2019-04-18/fact-check-can-algorithms-screen-out-hate-content-social-media/10979770.

4   Andrew Tillet, 'Social Media Chiefs Face Jail Terms', *Australian Financial Review*, March 26, 2019, at https://www.afr.com/politics/federal/social-media-chiefs-face-jail-terms-20190325-p5177e.

5   See Prime Minister's Media Release, March 30, 2019 at https://www.pm.gov.au/media/tough-new-laws-protect-australians-live-streaming-violent-crimes.

The Prime Minister Owes Cardinal Pell an Apology[1]

The High Court's unanimous acquittal of Cardinal George Pell, after two previous judicial rulings that failed to acknowledge a reasonable doubt as to the defendant's guilt, appears to indicate that the administration of justice in Australia has been corrupted by a desire to persecute and punish, not prosecute justly.

There has been a strong odour of miscarriage of justice about the whole matter. However, when Cardinal Pell was still awaiting trial, the Australian Prime Minister implied his guilt by making statements about those who 'abused the shield of faith and religion to hide their crimes shall stand condemned'.[2]

Before the High Court finally overruled the Cardinal's conviction, Scott Morrison stated: 'Our justice system has affirmed no Australian is above the law'. Mr Morrison also stated that 'the courts had done their work well'.[3]

According to criminal law professor Kenneth Arenson, there has been an "unsettling trend" in Victoria regarding to the introduction of laws that 'seriously impinge on the entrenched common law right of an accused to adduce all legally admissible and exculpatory evidence on his or her behalf'.[4]

However, before a final appeal had even been made to the nation's highest court, Mr Morrison had already started to look at taking action against Cardinal Pell.

The Prime Minister was especially interested in stripping Cardinal Pell of his Order of Australia honour. In fact, he vowed to the nation that Pell would lose his Order of Australia after Victoria's Court of Appeal upheld his guilty verdict.

As reported by Judith Ireland on August 12, 2019:

> *Mr Morrison said his sympathies were [solely] with the victims of sexual abuse... while Governor-General David Hurley said he would wait until Pell makes a decision about a possible appeal before "terminating" his prestigious Order of Australia... [He] told reporters in Canberra ... that the courts had "done their job" and must be respected. "They have rendered their verdict, and that's the system of justice in this country and that must be respected", he said, adding this would see Pell, who remains a cardinal of the church, lose his Order of Australia.*[5]

That being so, the Prime Minister's Office was already preparing to make an urgent application to the Council of the Order of Australia in order to have his appointment revoked. When informed that Cardinal Pell's lawyers were appealing to the High Court, Morrison dismissively commented: "I respect the fact that this case is under appeal, but it is the victims and their families I am thinking of today".[6]

In sum, Mr Morrison kept indirectly implying that Cardinal Pell was convicted of the crimes that the High Court has now found him to be entirely innocent.

Fortunately, Governor-General David Hurley showed a greater level of maturity and discernment than the Prime Minister, communicating that he would wait until Cardinal Pell's lawyers made a decision regarding a possible appeal before terminating his Order of Australia.

"Once all legal proceedings have run their course, the Council for the Order of Australia may make a recommendation to me as

Chancellor of the Order, which I will act on", the Governor-General said.

Pell was released from jail on April 7, 2020, and soon after the High Court quashed his convictions. He has always maintained his innocence. 'I have consistently maintained my innocence while suffering from a serious injustice', said Pell shortly after his acquittal was announced.

The fact that juries and courts in Australia can reach incorrect verdicts should not come as a surprise. There are notorious cases of wrongful convictions throughout Australia's court history, including Colin Campbell Ross, the Mickelberg brothers, Andrew Mallard, and, Lindy Chamberlain, considered arguably to be the greatest miscarriage of justice in Australia's history, to name only a few.

Had the Cardinal not enough support and money to appeal from his unjust conviction, he would be just another victim of a miscarriage of justice by the Australian court system.

The High Court ruling should invite a reflection on the Prime Minister's commitment to the presumption of innocence. After all, Mr Morrison has betrayed his pretence of Christian faith by raising false witness. He effectively pre-judged an innocent person, thus further inflating the anti-Catholic sentiment already prevalent in Australia, especially amongst its illiberal ruling groups.

The Prime Minister owes an apology not only to Cardinal Pell but also to every victim of false allegations and miscarriage of justice in Australia.

Chapter 7 endnotes

1   Based on: A. Zimmermann, 'Why ScoMo Owes Cardinal Pell an Apology (And to Every Victim of a Miscarriage of Justice in Australia), *Caldron Pool*, May 25, 2020, at https://caldronpool.com/why-scomo-owes-cardinal-pell-an-apology-and-to-every-victim-of-a-miscarriage-of-justice-in-australia/. Revised and updated by Prof Augusto Zimmermann and Dr Rocco Loiacono.

2   Calla Wahlquist, 'Scott Morrison Deeply Shocked by Pell Conviction Amid Calls to Strip Honours', *The Guardian*, February 26, 2019, at https://www.theguardian.com/australia-news/2019/feb/26/scott-morrison-deeply-shocked-by-pell-conviction-amid-calls-to-strip-honours.

3   NeosKosmos, 'PM Scott Morrison Is Looking To Strip Cardinal George Pell of his Order of Australia Honour', February 27, 2019, at https://neoskosmos.com/en/2019/02/27/news/australia/pm-scott-morrison-is-looking-to-strip-cardinal-george-pell-of-his-order-of-australia-honour/.

4   Kenneth J Arenson, 'The Demise of Equality Before the Law: The Pernicious Effects of Political Correctness in the Criminal Law of Victoria', (2016) 7 *The Western Australian Jurist* 1, at 61.

5   Judith Ireland, 'Scott Morrison Says George Pell Will Lose Order of Australia', *The Sydney Morning Herald*, August 21, 2019, at https://www.smh.com.au/politics/federal/scott-morrison-says-george-pell-will-lose-order-of-australia-20190821-p52j94.html.

6   Benjamin Preiss and Michael Koziol, 'Political Leaders Express Disgust at Abuse By Cardinal George Pell', *The Age*, February 6, 2019, at https://www.theage.com.au/national/victoria/political-leaders-express-disgust-at-abuse-by-cardinal-george-pell-20190226-p510fg.html.

Chapter 8

Morrison's Reckless Apology Puts Australians at Risk[1]

In early December 2020 a prominent Chinese official shared a fake image of an Australian Digger threatening to slit the throat of an Afghan child. In a tweet accompanying the fake image, Beijing's Foreign Industry spokesman said: "Shocked by the murder of Afghan civilians and prisoners by Australian soldiers, we strongly condemn such acts and call for holding them accountable". He also stated: "The Australian government should make a solemn promise to the international community that such atrocities will never happen again".[2]

Where did he get such a terrible idea from? From the Australian Prime Minister, of course.

Scott Morrison has falsely claimed that our defence forces serving in Afghanistan were murdering prisoners and innocent civilians. He announced in November 2020 that he had apologised to the President of Afghanistan for the contents of a report he hadn't even read.[3] Although these are only allegations and everyone should be given the presumption of innocence, the Prime Minister nonetheless declared that the alleged SAS war crimes in Afghanistan are "disturbing and distressing".[4]

Morrison has denied our soldiers the presumption of innocence. He has been shown to ignore completely the common-law principle that everyone is innocent until it can be proven otherwise. As the member for Curtin Celia Hammond stated in a speech to the Federal Parliament on November 30, 2020:

> We must avoid at all costs a situation where our defence forces are universally demonised. They are individual men and women who serve and sacrifice for us. Ultimately, it must never be us-versus-them because they are us.[5]

Of course, she is absolutely correct. And this is precisely what the Prime Minister has done. The world was listening and China heard these accusations by Morrison against our Australian Defence Forces.

It would not be unreasonable to argue that Morrison's accusations have dramatically empowered our enemies and increased the threat of Islamic terrorism on the Australian soil. As Sky News presenter Alan Jones pointed out:

> How extraordinary that we approve the unified condemnation of China's behaviour, but our Prime Minister can't find courage enough to accept the extent to which his language has defamed thousands of innocent, courageous and heroic Australians whom we sent to Afghanistan to put their lives on the line in our name.[6]

Alan Jones concludes: "Prime Minister, never mind asking the Chinese to apologise. You should apologise to the nation and the world".

I wholeheartedly agree with him. It is now patently clear that Morrison's ill-conceived remarks against our army personnel poses a serious threat to our national security. The Prime Minister has escalated the risk of terrorism by inviting radical Islamists to seek retaliation for the alleged crime of killing innocent Muslims in Afghanistan. He has defamed the nation and empowered our enemies.

Chapter 8 endnotes

1   Based on: A. Zimmermann, 'PM's Reckless Apology Puts Australians at Risk', *Caldron Pool*, December 4, 2020, at https://caldronpool.com/zimmermann-pms-reckless-apology-puts-australians-at-risk/. Revised and updated by Prof Augusto Zimmermann and Dr Rocco Loiacono.

2   'Australian Gov't Should Apologise to Afghan People: Chinese FM Spokesperson', *XinhuaNet*, June 25, 2021, at http://www.xinhuanet.com/english/2020-12/01/c_139553983.htm.

3   Andrew Greene, 'Afghanistan President Says Scott Morrison Called To Express Sorrow Ahead of War Crimes Report Release', ABC News, November 19, 2020, at https://www.abc.net.au/news/2020-11-19/afghanistan--scott-morrison-call-sorrow-war-crimes-report/12898574.

4   Andrew Greene, 'Alleged SAS War Crimes in Afghanistan are 'Disturbing and Distressing', Prime Minister Scott Morrison Says', ABC News, November 21, 2020, at https://www.abc.net.au/news/2020-11-21/scott-morrison-afghanistan-war-crimes-report-disturbing-distress/12907424.

5   Lanai Scarr, 'Don't Tar Australian Defence Force With Same Brush, Says Member for Curtin Celia Hammond', *The West Australian*, December 3, 2020, at https://thewest.com.au/politics/defence/dont-tar-australian-defence-force-with-same-brush-says-member-for-curtin-celia-hammond-ng-b881737523z.

6   Alan Jones, 'ScoMo owes us apology, not just China', *The Daily Telegraph*, December 2, 2020, at https://www.dailytelegraph.com.au/news/opinion/alan-jones-scott-morrison-gave-china-the-opening/news-story/caec157dc262a86f4eb3ea0f7f1f054f.

Part 2

RELIGIOUS FREEDOM

Chapter 9

We Need a Restoration of Freedoms Bill, Not Religious Discrimination Legislation[1]

The Morrison government has promised to introduce a religious discrimination bill. At the time of writing, a second draft of the bill was presented for consultation by Attorney-General, Senator Michaelia Cash. And yet, these reforms are unsatisfactory. They pose a further danger to freedom of speech and freedom of association.

There have been several statements from our Prime Minister which confirm his appalling lack of regard for freedom of speech. According to Morrison, "free speech doesn't create one job, doesn't open one business, doesn't give anyone one extra hour. It doesn't make housing more affordable or energy more affordable."[2]

In sum, he doesn't care much about basic freedoms just so long as everyone has a job. Isn't that remarkably similar to the way communists think?

Morrison strongly believes that we are a multicultural society where every religion deserves the same level of legal treatment and protection. In December 2018, he announced that further restrictions to free speech are necessary because of "Australia's booming multicultural communities, stressing that new arrivals tended to have strong religious beliefs and wanted those beliefs protected from harassment or intimidation".[3]

Apparently, Morrison upholds the false premise of moral equivalence between different religions, so that all religious values and practices are to be afforded the same level of legal protection from strong criticism and condemnation.

However, different religions uphold different values and produce different types of society. As stated by the Melbourne Anglican theologian, Dr Mark Durie:

> These differences extend to understandings of slavery, caste, marriage (e.g., monogamy, divorce, polygamy), the death penalty, euthanasia, the distribution of wealth, sexual politics, abortion, attitudes to truth, the nature of political representation, the whole legal system, and warfare. Treating religions as merely a matter of [cultural] identity is a recipe for confusion.[4]

The Prime Minister claims to be a Christian. And yet, he does not even support the right of a fellow believer to exercise free speech. On the contrary, when asked about Rugby Australia's controversial sacking of Wallabies star Israel Folau, Morrison stated: "I don't want religion to be a point of conflict in Australia".

As Paul Collits puts it "[his] failure to see the Folau case as a flagship freedom-of-speech issue is chilling for anyone with a modicum of understanding of how and why freedom is important".[5]

The Prime Minister should be reminded that it is simply impossible to protect any group's right to not be offended without grievously infringing on the constitutional freedom of political communication of others who strongly disagree with them.[6]

Australia is a society where people of different faiths and of no faith have to relate to one another and develop ways of living together. That being so, everyone should avoid being "uncomfortable" in robust conversations about religion. Indeed, the idea that any group should be sheltered from criticism is totally inimical to freedom of speech, which is a cardinal precept of every free and democratic society, and an indispensable shelter against totalitarianism. Indeed, freedom of speech was described in 1966 by Campbell and Whitmore as 'the freedom *par excellence*; for without it, no other freedom could survive'.[7]

In a liberal democracy, people must have the freedom to air unpopular views, including those informed by their faith, and those views must be open to challenge. However, the Morrison government's push for a religious discrimination act could provide a shield to religious extremists and advocates of principles offensive to our liberal democracy, such as blasphemy laws.

It seems, therefore, no mere coincidence that the Australian Federation of Islamic Councils (AFIC) is enthusiastically supporting the introduction of a religious discrimination law. AFIC president, Mr Rateb Jneid, argued that this Islamic organisation has been urging the federal government "to accept ... a religious freedom act," he told *The Australian* newspaper.[8]

I humbly suggest the president of the Islamic Councils begin his campaign for more religious freedom (other than Islam) in all of the countries in the Middle East except of course for the only democracy in the region – namely, Israel.

David Fawcett, in his capacity as chairman of the Parliamentary Inquiry into the Status of the Human Right to Freedom of Religion or Belief, stated: "While a culture of religious freedom has thrived, and the common law has respected religious freedom to a large extent, the legislative framework to ensure this continues is vulnerable."[9]

We agree with him. However, this would be far better guaranteed not by a religious discrimination act, but instead by a new law that restores free speech, freedom of conscience and freedom of association to every Australian citizen, religious or not, so we can all enjoy these fundamental rights.

Unveiling the government's long-awaited response to Philip Ruddock's religious freedom review in June 2019, the Prime

Minister promised a new 'Freedom of Religion Commissioner', despite Mr Ruddock recommending against such an office.

The introduction of a federal religious discrimination bill would make criticism of religion unlawful discrimination, and create a dangerously powerful statutory position of religious commissioner in the Australian Human Rights Commission. As the Institute of Public Affairs Morgan Begg correctly explained:

> *The current proposal from the Morrison government is to introduce a religious discrimination act and to establish the position of religious freedom commissioner within the Australian Human Rights Commission. Further details about these reforms are urgently needed, but the thought of the AHRC being given more laws to administer is a troubling prospect – given its history administering laws like section 18C of the Racial Discrimination Act there is sufficient reason to consider that a pessimistic prospect for freedom… A healthy liberal democracy depends on the good faith of its members to tolerate speech they may find disagreeable – and to disagree in open debate.*[10]

Although it is broadly accepted that religious freedom is increasingly vulnerable in Australia, we have serious doubts about the introduction of religious discrimination law that further impinges on free speech being the solution. As stated by the Australian Christian Lobby managing director, Martyn Iles:

> *The law firm I helped establish has handled more than 60 cases where Australians have lost their jobs, were stripped of their professional accreditations, were hauled up for hate speech, booted out of university, denied the right to be foster parents, and generally bullied every which way imaginable by activists wielding reams of legislation, backed by a discrimination commissioner with an Orwellian mindset.*
>
> *Meanwhile, the government is holding out a few shrivelled fig leaves to solve the problem — running away, as usual. On*

*offer is another anti-discrimination act (this time for religion)
and a review of exemptions to anti-discrimination laws to be
done by the Australian Law Reform Commission — no doubt
destined to say much, do little and ultimately gather dust in the
parliamentary library.*[11]

Where is the real answer?

First of all, there is no need to protect any religious group in
particular. Like ourselves, Mr Iles understands that a much better
way to proceed is to look at repealing the existing provisions in
anti-discrimination laws that seriously impinge on free speech and
freedom of association, in a way that strengthens the protection of
religious freedom and, in fact, attempts to ensure that the widest
scope of personal freedom is maintained when balancing conflicting
human rights.

Above all, nothing excuses undermining the basic rights of
some people in order to advance the supposed rights of others. And
yet, for the last twenty years or so anti-discrimination laws no doubt
have contributed to a remarkable muzzling of freedom of speech and
freedom of association.

The Morrison government would go a long way in protecting
religious freedom by restoring freedom of speech and freedom of
association in this country, rather than further undermining free
speech and equality before the law.

This may involve the enactment of a *Restoration of Freedoms Act*
that re-calibrates the relationship between the conflicting human
rights, and it does so by using language that does not suggest that
the freedom of religion (and criticism of religion) is an inferior or
secondary right.

Apart from a legislative act that restores free speech and freedom
of association for all, a law against the incitement of religious violence
would also do more good than one against religious discrimination,
in my opinion. But the Morrison government is clearly headed

in the wrong direction when it comes to the legal protection of fundamental rights and freedoms.

And let's not forget that the Liberal Party even dumped a conservative federal candidate in Victoria simply because he raised some concerns about radical Islam. Indeed, when this candidate dared to ask key questions about the link between radical Islam and terrorism without fear or favour, the ruling elite in the Victorian Liberal Party dismissed these concerns and accused him of anti-Muslim hatred or bigotry.

We need to inform the Prime Minister that we certainly don't support any further anti-discrimination laws, and this time on religious grounds. This would be going the wrong way in terms of upholding our individual rights and freedoms. Instead, we urge the Morrison government to pass a *Restoration of Freedoms Act*. This would involve federal legislation being enacted that fully restores the basic rights of all the Australian citizens to free speech, freedom of conscience, and freedom of association.

Chapter 9 endnotes

1   A Zimmermann, 'We Need a Restoration of Freedoms Bill, Not Religious Freedom Legislation', *The Spectator Australia*, July 3, 2019, at https://www.spectator.com.au/2019/07/we-need-a-restoration-of-freedoms-bill-not-religious-freedom-legislation. Revised and updated by Prof Augusto Zimmermann and Dr Rocco Loiacono.

2   Michael Koziol, 'Scott Morrison Warns Against Internal Fight Over Free Speech Laws: 'It Doesn't Create One Job'', *The Sydney Morning Herald*, March 1, 2017, at https://www.smh.com.au/politics/federal/scott-morrison-warns-against-internal-fight-over-free-speech-laws-it-doesnt-create-one-job-20170301-gunoqu.html.

3   Michael Koziol, 'Scott Morrison Pledges Religious Discrimination Act But Delays Protections For Gay Students', *The Sydney Morning Herald*, December 13, 2018, at https://www.smh.com.au/politics/federal/scott-morrison-pledges-religious-discrimination-act-but-delays-protections-for-gay-students-20181213-p5.

4   Mark Durie, 'Notes on *the Victorian Racial and Religious Tolerance Act (2001)*', Address at Seminar on Religious Tolerance Laws of the Christian Legal Society of Victoria (June 2, 2005).

5   Paul Collits, 'Why Israel Folau is Marked for Destruction', *Quadrant*, June 24, 2019, at https://quadrant.org.au/opinion/qed/2019/06/why-israel-folau-must-be-destroyed/.

6   See Joshua Forrester, Lorraine Finlay and Augusto Zimmermann, *No Offence Intended: Why 18C is Wrong* (Connor Court, 2016), 130.

7   Enid Campbell and Harry Whitmore, *Freedom in Australia* (Sydney University Press, 1966), 113.

8   Geoff Chambers and Joe Kelly, 'Muslims Want Protection in Religion Bill', *The Australian*, October 3, 2019, at https://www.theaustralian.com.au/nation/politics/muslims-want-protection-in-religion-bill/news-story/c5c4677261f6fd6f71a5951d743ee99b.

9   Joint Standing Committee on Foreign Affairs, Defence and Trade, Parliament of Australia, *Legal Foundations of Religious Freedom in Australia*, November 2017, p viii.

10 Morgan Begg, 'Legislating Free Speech', Institute of Public Affairs, June 28, 2019, at https://ipa.org.au/publications-ipa/legislating-free-speech.

11 Martyn Iles, 'Israel Folau: Voters Derail The PC Freight Train', *The Australian*, May 24, 2019, at https://www.theaustralian.com.au/business/legal-affairs/voters-derail-the-pc-freight-train/news-story/0f85b402b54bc29dd706f86c97b5b8c1.

Chapter 10

Religious Freedom Proposal is a Dud[1]

The Morrison government has been preparing a religious discrimination bill. However, these reforms are utterly unsatisfactory because they do not address, and in some cases compound, the unconstitutionality of "hate speech" laws. Some of these laws, such as the notorious section 18C of the *Racial Discrimination Act* (Cth) and equivalent provisions in the states and territories, impermissibly infringe the implied constitutional freedom of political communication.

Any reform should not use the language of discrimination but actually put Australia in line with its international human rights obligations to protect religious freedom. Adding an additional protected "class" of religious people and organisations does not overcome the problems with respect to those classes that legal provisions currently cover.

If anything, adding a new class of protected individuals compounds the problem of the constitutional invalidity of laws that may already unreasonably impinge on the freedoms of religion and political communication.

What is more, according to Patrick Parkinson, law dean at the University of Queensland, "the religious discrimination bill, as the government envisages it, will have no impact whatsoever on vilification law in the states. All it will do is make it unlawful under federal law to discriminate against somebody because of their faith."

A religious discrimination act "would not solve all or even most of the problems with religious freedom in Australia", Parkinson says.

If that is the case, then such legislation could be construed in such a way as to still allow the states to take action against religious leaders over the public dissemination of doctrine that leaves people feeling offended.

The free exercise of religion is a fundamental freedom that is protected by section 116 of the Australian Constitution. Courts have also found an implied freedom of political communication, which includes as a corollary freedom of association. These freedoms must also cover, by logical extension, religious people and religious organisations.

The International Covenant on Civil and Political Rights ("ICCPR") supports these constitutional freedoms. It was signed by Australia in 1972 and its protection for freedom of religion is found in article 18, which is primarily concerned with the right to "freedom of thought, conscience and religion" but it also encompasses the right to "adopt a religion or belief".

An infringement of fundamental rights protected by article 18 of the ICCPR, such as freedom of religion, may also simultaneously involve the infringement of the right to privacy (article 17), the right to peaceful assembly (article 21), the right to freedom of association (article 22), and the right to the equal protection of the law without discrimination (article 26).

The Morrison government has a legal and moral responsibility to adhere to Australia's international human rights obligations. Having endorsed the ICCPR and other international law instruments, this government is obligated to use its legislative powers to support Australia's constitutional freedoms. It should protect not only religious freedom but freedom of speech, freedom of conscience, freedom of association and the right to peaceful assembly.

This can be done because the High Court has generally adopted an expansive approach to the external affairs power found in the

Australian Constitution. This power, wrote chief justice Harry Gibbs in the *Tasmanian Dam* Case (1983), subjects the federal government to "no significant limits", thus offering a potential to invalidate state law in virtually every respect regarding any infringements of religious freedom.

Unfortunately, the proposed religious discrimination act appears to be a missed opportunity.

If the government does not reform the existing laws to remove constitutionally invalid restrictions on religious freedom and its correlating freedom of speech and freedom of association (for religious people or not), we can only hope that an Australian state will know it should and can take the initiative to restore our fundamental rights and freedoms, and pay proper respect to the Constitution.

Chapter 10 endnotes

1   A Zimmermann, 'Religious Freedom Proposal is a Dud', *The Australian*, July 12, 2019, at https://www.theaustralian.com.au/business/legal-affairs/religious-freedom-proposal-is-a-dud/news-story/c1cf0b6ad9c8011eff158d7650e95bc8. Revised and updated by Prof Augusto Zimmermann and Dr Rocco Loiacono.

A Religious Freedom Commissioner: Not Just Worse Than Doing Nothing, But The Wrong Thing[1]

Unveiling the government's long-awaited response to Philip Ruddock's religious freedom review, Scott Morrison promised in July 2019 a new 'Freedom of Religion Commissioner', despite Ruddock and his team explicitly recommending against such an office.

Speaking to *Guardian Australia*, the then Attorney General Christian Porter stated that such legislation would include a clause relating to indirect discrimination, mirrored on section 7b of the *Sex Discrimination Act*. He believed that such a provision could prevent employers from putting in place a binding condition on all employees that restrict their expression of religious views.

The *Sex Discrimination Act* is invariably used against men. The *Racial Discrimination Act* is invariably used against white people. We can therefore only guess against whom the *Religious Discrimination Act* will be used. The problem is aggravated by the fact that the government intends to establish the position of religious freedom commissioner in the Australian Human Rights Commission.

Writing for *The Australian*, Angela Shanahan believes that this is about "widening the power of the identity-obsessed elites trying to set up competing ideas of human rights, defined and policed by the growing power of extra-parliamentary instruments such as the Australian Human Rights Commission".[2] She argues that such an idea is intrinsically anti-democratic and it can potentially further undermine human rights.

Shanahan cites the case in Tasmania of Catholic Archbishop Julian Porteous, who was brought to a similar commission simply because he authorised the distribution of a very mild booklet that expresses the Church's respect for the dignity of homosexuals, while at the same time promoting the goodness of traditional marriage and why children are adversely affected if they miss out on a mother and father. According to her, that case in Tasmania demonstrates that such commissions are not used to necessarily protect "real" human rights. "These commissions have been used to actually narrow our rights", she says.

Some Christian organisations put submissions into the Ruddock Review calling for the establishment of a religious freedom commissioner. However, this could completely backfire and we would go so far as to state that such an idea is extremely dangerous. These organisations naively believe that the answer to the problems created by discrimination laws is to ask for more such laws. And then they trust the government, which has shown no interest to protect free speech and freedom of association, to protect these rights of Christians to discriminate against others on the grounds of religious convictions.

In recent years this country has experienced a dramatic restriction of freedom of speech, most often in the name of encouraging "tolerance" and "responsible" public debate. If a 2012 bill introduced by the then Labor government had been passed, the scope of discrimination laws would have been considerably expanded. As a result, greater restrictions on free speech would be imposed at the same time that procedural burdens on respondents seeking to defend themselves would be decreased.

The scheme outlined was so draconian that it even reversed the onus of the proof. The burden of proof would rest with those who had been charged rather than staying with those who felt offended or humiliated by any particular statement. According to Simon Breheny, "[t]hat such a dangerous and draconian legislation could even have been contemplated in a free and democratic country such as Australia is alarming ... No less alarming is that the bill was enthusiastically supported by the Australian Human Rights Commission".[3]

This is the same organisation that the government is just about to confer further powers on so as to define matters of religion and religious discrimination. We can easily predict that, once such a position is created, it would only be a matter of time before some unorthodox Church leader is appointed as the religious freedom commissioner in this Commission. Based on his or her "creative" understanding of the Christian faith, this person would be most tempted to make an authoritative decision that statements such as "marriage is between a man and a woman" are not protected under religious freedom laws because such a statement is no longer universally held by Christian denominations.

Muslims, of course, would be legally protected in their rights to discriminate against homosexuals, because they are a so-called "discriminated minority" and such a statement is in full conformity with Islamic doctrine.

Then the 'exemptions' for Christians would be removed by further legislation. And then the federal courts would follow precedent of the *Racial Discrimination Act* and find that statements against Christians do not constitute vilification because Christianity is arguably not a minority religion in Australia.

And then all that would be left is a law that protects a few minorities chosen by the identity-possessed political and intellectual elites to be the recipients of special legal privileges, but not the majority Christian population.

Michael Stead, Anglican Bishop of South Sydney, reminds us that the issue has been falsely construed by the government as a right of religious people and organisations to discriminate on the basis of religious values and convictions. In other words, such a debate is being inaccurately construed as a religious "right to be a bigot".

However, as Bishop Stead correctly points out, Christians don't want the right to discriminate against anybody. The right that they want is that of expressing their belief in public "and for that not to be caught up in anti-discrimination law". He is quite correct to comment that the Morrison government should "move the debate away from discrimination".

Unfortunately this is the opposite of what the government intends to do. Rather than expanding the scope of unelected bodies and creating more discrimination laws, the Morrison government should enact legislation that would give effect to Australia's international obligations to protect religious freedom and in the context of other fundamental rights of the individual, including free speech, freedom of association, freedom of conscience, and the right to peaceful assembly.

In this sense, handing over the definition of religion to the Human Rights Commission is a terrible idea that risks further undermining our individual rights and freedoms. Wanting to be seen to do something, this government is just about to hand over a vast array of powers to a controversial body of unelected lawyers that have an appalling record of disregard for freedom of speech.

Although it is broadly accepted that religious freedom is increasingly vulnerable in Australia, we have serious doubts about the desirability of more discrimination law that further impinges on freedom of speech. Of course, we must be able to exercise the democratic right to freely talk about religion and to criticise any religion whatsoever. And yet, this is not exactly what the Morrison government is considering to do, and quite to the contrary.

Worse than doing nothing is to actually end up doing the wrong thing.

Our opinion is based upon the view of the High Court as stated in several of its landmark decisions. Overall, these decisions inform that our system of representative government requires every citizen to be entitled to communicate in a free and open manner about matters of a political nature, including when these matters may be intertwined with a critical analysis or scrutiny of religious beliefs and practices.

The implied freedom of political communication is a constitutional principle introduced by the High Court in the early 1990s. This important freedom prevents the government from disproportionately restricting freedom of speech. Based primarily upon the view that the system of representative and responsible government was established by the Constitution, the implied freedom requires that the people and their representatives must be able to communicate in a free and open manner about political matters.

The provision derived from Section 18C of the *Racial Discrimination Act* is particularly unconstitutional because it is not supported by the external affairs power in s 51(xxix) of the Constitution, with such provision reaching well beyond the intended scope of the *International Convention on the Elimination of All Forms of Racial Discrimination*. For instance, international law does not recognise the right to not be offended. The second is that s 18C impermissibly infringes upon the freedom of communication about government and political matters implied from the Constitution.

Now it is the freedom to politically communicate on religious matters that is further at risk. The Grand Mufti of Australia, Dr Ibrahim Abu Mohamed, has notoriously called on Scott Morrison to push for new laws to greater protect Muslims against so-called "Islamophobia"; that is, the strong criticism of the Islamic religion.

This is confirmed by a leaked video of the Prime Minister meeting with Dr Mohamed and other Islamic leaders at Lakemba Mosque. The video shows Morrison being warmly welcomed by the Muslim leadership and urged by them to extend section 18C to religious grounds. At the same meeting, the Muslim Association Director, Ahmad Malas, demanded the Prime Minister review all federal laws to address "the need for the Government to take responsibility at stamping out the ideology of white supremacy".[4]

The Australian Grand Mufti notoriously states that section 18C should be amended to allow Muslims to receive the same level of legal protection afforded to ethnic groups. Let us remember that this is the same leader who has criticised a secular judge (Justice Fagan of the NSW Supreme Court) for daring to ask why these leaders often fail to disavow the "belligerent" verses of the Koran, thus weakening the convictions of Islamic terrorists.

Justice Fagan made a fair comment, particularly with regard to the apparent reliance on Koranic verses to support a duty of religious violence as a fact that has been testified in a number of cases across Australia. If the verses upon which terrorists rely are not the binding commands of the god of Islam, then, Justice Fagan concluded, "it is Muslims who would have to say so".

The opinion of this judge was met with profound indignation by the Grand Mufti. Dr Mohammed was adamant that Koranic verses can never be criticised by whoever the person might be, including the verses in the Koran that promote anti-Semitism and religious violence. "This will never happen", he said menacingly, before accusing that judge of being "uninformed" about the real teachings of the Koran: "You don't ask to disavow medicine if some doctors exploit it, you don't ask to disavow law if some judge misuses it", Dr Mohammed said.

In the exercise of his role as the nation's primary Muslim leader, Dr Mohammed has met several times with Morrison. Dr Mohammed recently visited him in order to request 'the introduction of new laws which would make it an offence to discriminate against Muslims'. Dr Mohammed took the opportunity to issue the following warning to the Prime Minister:

> We are waiting for the response of the two big parties, the prime minister and the opposition leader ... and we know that hate and racism are incidental viruses to [Australia's] society. Everyone, Muslim or non-Muslims, no matter what colour they are, we are all guests on Aboriginal land.[5]

One cannot hide the irony that, in their attempt to prevent themselves from ever feeling offended, such religious leaders have no qualms in deeply offending the country's majority ethnic group. Having arrived in our democratic society, many Muslims escaping from remarkably oppressive theocratic regimes start to develop a visceral hatred for the ethnic majority that have so generously received them in our tolerant community, and not so often as refugees from their native Islamic nations.

As for the claim that we are all guests on Aboriginal land, if the same rationale were applied to the countries of Northern Africa (and even most of the countries in the Middle East), then all Muslims living in these parts of the world should consider themselves to be guests on Christian lands. Of course, Islam only became the dominating religion in Northern Africa after many centuries of violence, slavery and ultimately the genocide of the original Christian inhabitants of these conquered lands. And even to this very day Islamists attack and kill Christians in the Middle East and Northern Africa, and burn down their places of worship.

Above all, we should resist the idea that any legislative reform should be used to protect Muslims from feeling offended by means of criticism or rejection of their religion. Instead, we must strive to put Australia in line with its international human rights obligations to protect religious freedom in the context of free speech, freedom of conscience, freedom of association, and the right to peaceful assembly.

The Morrison government has under international law the legal (and moral) duty to adhere to Australia's international human rights obligations. Furthermore, the free exercise of religion is a fundamental freedom of the individual that is legally protected by Section 116 of the Australian Constitution. Courts have also found an implied freedom of political communication, which includes as a corollary freedom of association.

These freedoms must be extended, by logical extension, to religious people and religious organisations. Adding religious people as an additional "class" of protected people further compounds the problem of the constitutional invalidity of laws that may already unreasonably impinge the freedom of political communication. On this count, the changes proposed by these Islamic groups are constitutionally invalid.

Because religious freedom is not the only human right, the question of the relationship between different fundamental rights arises. Article 18 of the ICCPR specifies that 'only such limitations as are prescribed by law and are necessary to protect public safety, order, health or morals or the fundamental rights and freedoms of others'. Religious freedom can therefore be limited on grounds of national security and broader protection of fundamental human rights for all. That being so, writes Centre for Independent Studies Senior Fellow and retired Anglican Bishop Robert Forsyth:

> As important as the right to religious liberty is, it is crucial to add that protecting it should not entail any laws that remove others' rights to criticise, deny or even ridicule any particular religious belief or practice ... Therefore, it is essential to rule out any notion that blasphemy should be either reintroduced or reinvigorated as an offence. Nor can religious freedom protection guarantee that religious points of view will

necessarily be listened to, or religious leaders respected in public debate. These are matters properly outside the reach of law in liberal democracies.[6]

Adrienne Stone of the University of Melbourne Law School notes that religious speech is in its nature quite often intertwined with "political opinions, perspectives, philosophies and practices".[7] Similarly, law professor Nicholas Aroney of the University of Queensland comments that, indeed, "religion, religious beliefs and religious practices (as well as irreligious beliefs) not infrequently inform, or are tied up with, political perspectives, philosophies and practices".[8]

Indeed, in *Evans v State of New South Wales* (2008) the Full Court of the Federal Court argued that "religious beliefs and doctrines frequently attract public debate and sometimes have political consequences reflected in government laws and policies". In *Adelaide Company of Jehovah's Witnesses Incorporated v The Commonwealth*, Latham CJ noted with respect to religious beliefs:

> *Such beliefs are concerned with the relation between man and the God whom he worships, although they are also concerned with the relation between man and the civil government under which he lives. They are political in character, but they are none the less religious on that account.* [emphasis added][9]

If religious and political matters are so often intertwined, then one must conclude that any logical derivation to the limitation imposed on freedom of religious communication amounts to a violation of the broader protection to freedom of political communication implied in the Australian Constitution.

In other words, since views about religion may so very well influence government policies through Australia's constitutionally-prescribed system of representative and responsible government, Section 116's constitutional protection of the free exercise of religion should also encompass communicating and associating about a religion's view on government or political matters.

If such a demand were to be attended, then the final outcome would be to outlaw our constitutional freedom of political communication if such communication may be displeasing to the inflated sensitivities of radical religionists. As David Crowe points out in the *Sydney Morning Herald*, "The obvious danger is a blasphemy law – if not in name, then in effect. At what point does speaking out against a religion turn into a form of discrimination that should be stopped?"[10]

Of course, there is no apparent reason as to why speech about religious matters should not be characterized as political communication to be protected by the (constitutional) freedom of political communication. Arguably, the push to protect people from strong criticism of their religion could provide a legal shield to religious extremists (jihadists) to freely advocate for a religious war against the West, or to promote without due criticism extremist religious ideas which are deeply offensive to the more tolerant and inclusive values of our democratic society.

From a more strictly moral point of view, it is a self-evident truth that no law should ever forbid the strong criticism of religion. After all, some religions actually deserve to be criticised, perhaps for embracing a theological perspective that fundamentally violates the fundamental rights and freedoms that we share so much in our tolerant and pluralistic society.

Above all, we should never allow our fundamental rights and freedoms to be undermined by the inflated sensitivities of any religious group, whatever this group might be. In a true democracy, everyone must be entitled to criticise religion, and to have the right to consider any form of religious manifestation ultimately retrograde and a potential threat to the preservation of a tolerant and pluralistic society.

Chapter 11 endnotes

1   Based on the articles: A Zimmermann, 'A Religious Freedom Commissioner: Not Just Worse Than Doing Nothing, But The Wrong Thing', *The Spectator Australia*, July 19, 2019, at https://www.spectator.com.au/2019/07/a-religious-freedom-commissioner-not-just-worse-than-doing-nothing-but-the-wrong-thing/. Revised and updated by Prof Augusto Zimmermann and Dr Rocco Loiacono; and A Zimmermann, 'The Religious Freedom Trojan Horse', *The Spectator Australia*, August 5, 2019, at https://www.spectator.com.au/2019/08/the-religious-freedom-trojan-horse/. Revised and updated by Prof Augusto Zimmermann and Dr Rocco Loiacono.

2   Angela Shanahan, 'Freedom of Religious Bill Could Be Misused By Greens, Far Left', *The Australian*, June 8, 2019, at https://www.theaustralian.com.au/inquirer/freedom-of-religion-bill-could-be-misused-by-greens-far-left/news-story/0d8830fde3cc8e84f3 1f4a720a60aa1a.

3   Simon Breheny, 'The Case for Changing Section 18C of the Radical Discrimination', Upholding the Australian Constitution, Samuel Griffith Society, Volume 26, 2014, p 115.

4   Avani Dias, 'Leaked Video Shows Islamic Leaders Calling on Scott Morrison For Protection Against Hate Speech', ABC Triple J, March 21, 2019, at https://www.abc.net.au/triplej/programs/hack/islamic-leaders-scott-morrison-hate-speech-christchurch/10925660.

5   Abdallah Kamal, 'Grand Mufti Class For Laws to Protect Muslims Against the Virus of Islamophobia', *SBS Arabic*, March 18, 2019, at https://www.sbs.com.au/language/english/grand-mufti-calls-for-laws-to-protect-muslims-against-the-virus-of-islamophobia.

6   Robert Forsyth, 'A Test of Maturity: Liberal Case for Action on Religious Freedom', The Centre for Independent Studies – Policy Paper N.8, August 2018, p 5.

7   Adrienne Stone, 'Rights, Personal Rights and Freedoms: The Nature of the Freedom of Political Communication' (2001) 25 *Melbourne University Law Review* 374, 386-87.

8   Nicholas Aroney, 'The Constitutional (In)Validity of Religious Vilification Laws: Implications For Their Interpretation' (2006) 34 *Federal Law Review* 288, p 306.

9   [1943] HCA 12; (1943) 67 CLR 116.

10 David Crowe, 'Religious discrimination laws are a new culture war in the making', *Sydney Morning Herald*, 4 July 2019, at https://www.smh.com.au/politics/federal/religious-discrimination-laws-are-a-new-culture-war-in-the-making-20190704-p5243k.html.

Part 3

DISCRIMINATION ISSUES

Dear Prime Minister, Australia is Not a Racist Country[1]

Australia is widely recognised as one of the most tolerant and ethnically diverse nations on the planet. There is absolutely nothing in our legal system that gives ground to the premise that we are an inherently racist nation.

However, when asked if Australia had a problem with racism, our Prime Minister did not reject such a premise. Rather, he went on simply to state that he was "truly sorry" at the treatment of Indigenous Australians over the years and by previous Australian governments.

As he marked the 13th anniversary of Kevin Rudd's apology for the Stolen Generations, Scott Morrison reiterated the historical apology delivered by the newly elected Labor government in 2008 after being resisted by the Howard government.

The Prime Minister told the House of Representatives on February 15, 2021: "I repeat the words of my predecessor, Mr Rudd: I am sorry. Truly sorry".[2]

Of course, it is rather inappropriate to expect Australians that have nothing to do with the alleged wrongdoings of the past to feel guilty and ashamed. Do we hold contemporary Germans and Japanese responsible for war crimes committed by other individuals more than 80 years ago?

We don't think so. After all, we should never make people feel guilty of the mistakes made by others in the distant past.

Such apologising is not only self-righteous and insincere but also prolongs the "victimisation culture" which has caused incredible pain and suffering for the Indigenous peoples of Australia. However, the Prime Minister has explicitly condemned all previous Australian governments, claiming that their policies have invariably caused "endless pain that cascaded through generations".

"Children forcibly removed from parents ... Siblings separated. Adoptions without consent... Actions of brute force carried out under claims of "good intentions" but in truth betrayed the ignorance of arrogance, 'knowing better than our Indigenous peoples", Morrison stated.[3]

Despite the danger of such broad emotional generalisations, no mention was made of the many wonderful foster parents who reared "stolen children" with utmost love and affection, thus making their lives fruitful and free from the chronic abuse and violence of some dysfunctional communities.

Arguably, the inflexible approach taken by the Prime Minister might potentially keep some Indigenous Australians from reaching their full potential. This can be found, for example, in the practice of placing Aboriginal children in need of care with "culturally appropriate" carers. "This practice has sometimes ended in tragedy", argues Dr Anthony Dillon, an Australian academic who identifies himself as part-Indigenous. Because of policies that prevent the adoption of Indigenous children by non-Indigenous foster parents, Dillon comments:

> Some children have suffered, all in the name of "culture". A colour-blind culture or way of life, characterised by love is a far more important consideration than a culture that is assumed to be Aboriginal simply because the adult potential carers themselves have some Aboriginal ancestry.[4]

The Prime Minister has also stated in Parliament: "Reconciliation will be achieved in this country only when young

Indigenous boys and girls can grow up with the same opportunities as every other Australian". However, the "endless pain" of Indigenous Australians is not caused from any lack of public assistance and funding. After all, around $850 billion has been spent since 1970 on grounds of improving the Aboriginal condition.

According to the Productivity Commission, Australian governments have spent more than double per person on services for Indigenous citizens than for other citizens. The ratio of indigenous to non-indigenous expenditure per head of population is 3:1 in school education; 4.9: 1 in public and community health services, and 4.85:1 in housing.

As can be seen, generous public funding has not been enough to close the gap between Indigenous and non-Indigenous Australians. However, due to the nature of Australia's politics, one runs the serious risk of being "cancelled" for merely stating this undeniable truth. As Dillon also points out, "when discussing Aboriginal matters there seems to be no end to where offence can be taken and accusations of racism made".

Therefore, it might be necessary for me to clarify that I do not object my fellow Australian citizens of Indigenous heritage from embracing, practicing or celebrating their culture, so long as it does not violate the fundamental legal rights of others and it is within the confines of the rule of law.

Instead, this short opinion piece is about a Prime Minister who believes that Australia is a racist country. Nothing can be further from the truth. Indeed, to suggest that any group of Australians actually needs some form of special protection from the depredations of other fellow citizens is not just deeply condescending but also profoundly fallacious.

Chapter 12 endnotes

1   Based on: A Zimmermann, 'Dear Prime Minister, Australia Is Not a Racist Country', *The Spectator Australia*, February 26, 2021, at https://www.spectator.com.au/2021/02/dear-prime-minister-australia-is-not-a-racist-country/. Revised and updated by Prof Augusto Zimmermann and Dr Rocco Loiacono.

2   Greg Brown, 'I'm Truly Sorry For The Endless Pain Of The Stolen Generations, Says Scott Morrison', *The Australian*, February 15, 2021, at https://www.theaustralian.com.au/nation/politics/im-truly-sorry-for-the-endless-pain-of-the-stolen-generations-says-scott-morrison/news-story/82522fc331ce5f43dd630c39ff7052c6.

3   'Statement on the Anniversary of the National Apology to the Stolen Generations', Prime Minister of Australia, Canberra, ACT, February 15, 2021, at https://www.pm.gov.au/media/statement-anniversary-national-apology-stolen-generations.

4   Anthony Dillon, 'Recognising May Mean Never Closing the Gap', *in* Gary Johns (ed.) *Recognise What? Arguments to Acknowledge Aboriginal Culture or rights, in the Australian Constitution* (Connor Court, 2014), p 61.

Menzies's Message for Morrison: "Gender Quotas Are Unfair and Illiberal"[1]

While Australians are worried about rising unemployment and exorbitant electricity bills, the government is concerned about "gender balance."

Prime Minister Scott Morrison says he is deeply committed to boosting female representation in the Liberal Party, and is pushing for structural reforms to his party to improve such representation in Parliament.[2]

First of all, the idea that the Liberal Party needs to have more female representation in Parliament is a misuse of language. After all, every member of Parliament is supposed to represent Australian men and women alike.

The premise that only a woman can truly represent the interests of women is not only is absurdly sexist but was discredited when Foreign Affairs Minister Marise Payne claimed she had "yet to speak to her Qatar counterpart" about the invasive internal examinations Qatari authorities subjected 13 Australian women to in Doha in October 2020.

However, Payne and other Liberal MPs, including Karen Andrews, Sussan Ley, Melissa Price, and Katie Allen, have seized on Morrison's support for gender quotas, and are calling for greater female representation in Parliament.

Curiously, there is no push for gender quotas in other "exciting" employment areas where women are massively underrepresented. Rarely can women be found in the fields of garbage collection, grave digging, and road construction.

Their fixation on gender quotas indicates these MPs are potentially taking the Liberal Party down the same path of identity politics as the Australian Labor Party, only more slowly.

Currently, about 50 percent of Labor MPs are female. How is that working for them? The ALP lost the last federal election and received around 300,000 fewer votes from women than the Liberal Party did.

Morrison and his colleagues in Parliament should think twice before dishonouring the founder of the Liberal Party by upholding such a divisive agenda.

As his main biographer David Furse-Roberts points out, Sir Robert Menzies distanced himself from the view of affirmative action feminists who argued that women should be promoted merely by virtue of the fact that they were women.[3]

Furse-Roberts also explains that, to Menzies, such an attitude was deficient because it "overlooked the personal merits and talents of the individual female candidate."

Calling for "better treatment" of women, current Prime Minister Morrison said, "I want women to have at least the same opportunities and the same voice and the same safety as men in this country."

Surely, a competent and capable woman would have no need for such rhetoric to advance her life and career?

Menzies would be appalled to see what the Prime Minister and these Liberal Party MPs with a small "l" are doing to the party he created.

He regarded it as profoundly unfair and indeed a great absurdity to claim a person's gender as a qualification to become a Liberal MP.

David Furse-Roberts holds a PhD in history from the University of New South Wales and is a research fellow at the Menzies Research Centre. His book *Menzies: The Forgotten Speeches* has an entire chapter on the "Status and Role of Women."

The first section in the chapter, entitled Women for Canberra, is based on a broadcast delivered by Menzies on January 29, 1943. There, Australia's longest serving prime minister said:

> *Of course, women are at least the equals of men. Of course, there is no reason why a qualified woman should not sit in Parliament, or on the bench, or in a professional chair, or preach from the pulpit, or, if you like, command an army in the field. No educated man today denies a place or a career to a woman because she is a woman.*

> *But there is a converse proposition which I state with all respect but with proper firmness. No woman can demand a place or a career just because she is a woman. If it is outmoded and absurd to treat a woman's sex as a political disqualification; it seems to me equally absurd to claim it as a qualification in itself ...*

> *For myself, I declined to vote for any woman just because she is a woman, but I will vote for her with no prejudice and with great cheerfulness if I am satisfied that she is, in the homely phrase, "the better man of the two."*

> *For, like most electors, I am not half so interested in the sex or social position or worldly wealth of my representatives and rulers as I am in the quality of their minds, the soundness of their characters, the humanity of their experience, the sanity of their policy, and the strength of their wills.*[4]

Years later, in a 1958 address to the Conference of the Headmistresses' Association of Australia, Menzies re-affirmed his opposition to the idea of gender quota:

> *It is true that over these many years women have played a small part in Parliament. We have had a few women in Parliament;*

not very many compared to the great body of Parliament. It has been a small part and you may say to me, "Why does that happen?" Some of you … will say to me, "That is the fault of men. They won't have women in Parliament". To which I reply: "There are more women on the [electoral] rolls than there are men in Australia, and if women are not in Parliament more than they are, it is because women don't vote for them!"

Now why? Well, I think it is explainable. I have myself, on more than one occasion, listened to a woman candidate for Parliament who stood up and made it her great policy speech to say, "I am a woman. The woman's point of view ought to be represented." If I were to stand up and say in Kooyong (which through sheer animadvertence does me the honour of returning me to Parliament), "I am a man and the man's point of view ought to be listened to," they would think I had become a little odd.

I have frequently had to say to my female political friends, "Look, don't ask people to vote for you because you are a woman. Ask them to vote for you because you are the best person in the field. You are the one to represent them. You are the one who will understand public problems."

But to say, "I think the woman's point of view should be represented, the woman's point of view being, with infinite respect, as elusive as a man's point of view, since who knows it – there are thousands of different points of view. That kind of statement is not an expression of equality, because if equality ought to be expressed there would be no occasion to say either, "I am a man," or "I am a woman." It is rather an expression of nervousness and uncertainty.[5]

As can be seen, advocating gender quotas was entirely anachronistic to Menzies' classical liberal philosophy.

Clearly, he would completely abhor modern identity politics, and the leftist agenda of gender quotas in particular.

Mark Powell reminds us in *The Spectator* that quotas for women in Parliament "stem from the creation of Emily's List by the Labor Left in 1994"—a progressive network supporting women seeking political office.

So, how can the modern Liberal Party dishonour Menzies' legacy by promising to introduce gender quotas that will surely result in unfair treatment based on gender?

It is quite simple. These individuals are not true Liberals in the sense conceived by Menzies. Indeed, according to Powell, "Menzies was deeply concerned as to how the left had started to infiltrate the party he had founded."[6]

As Maurice Newman wrote in *The Australian*:

> *Lest there be any doubt about Menzies' philosophy, it is clearly expressed in a 1974 letter lamenting that the state executive is dominated by what we now call Liberals with a small "l"—that is to say who believe in nothing, but who believe in anything if they think it is worth a few votes. The whole thing is tragic.*[7]

It goes without saying that Morrison's beliefs on the supposed unequal treatment of women should be challenged.

Affirmative action policies, like quotas, tend to leave job applicants with the same experience and qualifications disadvantaged.

Meanwhile, discrimination against white male applicants has become increasingly widespread, occurring in both blue-collar and professional contexts.

Laws make their employment increasingly more difficult. Australian white men swell the ranks of the homeless, and the prison population.

Most of these depressing statistics apply particularly to white working-class men—far more than any other ethnic or gender group. These are men who have lost their place in society and have no encouraging narrative to advance their life.

Despite these sobering realities and statistics, railing against "white male privilege" continues to be the rallying cry of those who control the mainstream media, academia, and politics.

Of course, one would still expect the party founded by Menzies to pre-select candidates solely on the basis of merit, and regardless of gender.

There is also a fine irony in the fact that such gender quotas are now being considered precisely when the New Left cannot even define the word "woman."

Chapter 13 endnotes

1   Based on: A Zimmermann, 'Menzies Had a Message for Morrison: Gender Quotas as Unfair and Illiberal', *The Epoch Times,* March 28, 2021, at https://www.theepochtimes.com/menzies-had-a-message-for-morrison-gender-quotas-are-unfair-and-illiberal_3751593.html. Revised and updated by Prof Augusto Zimmermann and Dr Rocco Loiacono.

2   Rosie Lewis and Geoff Chambers, 'Abuse of Women Must Stop: Scott Morrison', *The Australian,* March 24, 2021, at https://www.theaustralian.com.au/nation/politics/abuse-of-women-must-stop-scott-morrison/news-story/17beb05faa76d79f8cd455180e2d1548.

3   David Furse-Roberts (ed.), *Menzies: The Forgotten Speeches* (Jeparit Press, 2017), 245.

4   Sir Robert Menzies, 'Women for Canberra, Broadcast (29 January 1943)', in David Furse-Roberts (ed.), *Menzies: The Forgotten Speeches* (Jeparit Press, 2017), 246-47.

5   Sir Robert Menzies, 'Women in the Community – Present and Future', in David Furse-Roberts (ed.), *Menzies: The Forgotten Speeches* (Jeparit Press, 2017), 253-54.

6   Mark Powell, 'Menzies, Malcolm, Misogyny and Merit', *The Spectator Australia,* March 13, 2019, at https://www.spectator.com.au/2019/03/menzies-malcolm-misogyny-and-merit/.

7   Maurice Newman, 'Menzies Had a Word for Turnbull: It Wasn't Liberal', *The Australian,* December 4, 2018, at https://www.theaustralian.com.au/commentary/opinion/menzies-had-a-word-for-turnbull-it-wasnt-liberal/news-story/45f9939f7a8d622eb58d03d465dfc407.

Chapter 14

The Morrison Government's Demonisation of Australian Men[1]

The Morrison government promised in February 2019 to spend $78 million in taxpayers' money to protect women from family violence by Australian men. "Our government is fully engaged in working together to combat violence against women. It must stop", Scott Morrison said in an extract of a speech delivered on February 11, 2019.

How about helping men and children deal with violent women as well? According to the American sociology professor Stephen Baskerville:

> *Feminists portray domestic violence as a political crime perpetrated exclusively by men to, again, perpetrate male power. Yet the fact that men and women commit violent acts in the home in roughly equal numbers has been clearly established in so many studies that it requires no reiteration.*[2]

The most cursory scrutiny reveals that the "epidemic" of domestic violence is significantly fabricated. None of the statistics purporting to quantify a problem of domestic violence is based on convictions through jury trials or even formal charges. These accusations are based on "reports" that are not necessarily "substantiated", and substantial incentives exist for women and government-funded interest groups and government agencies to manufacture false accusations and exaggerate incidents.

For instance, there is an intrinsic connection between domestic violence accusations and the increase in divorce and child custody. Indeed, it is common knowledge among legal practitioners that unsubstantiated accusations are routinely used, and seldom punished, in divorce and custody proceedings. In other words, open perjury is readily acknowledged and, as a consequences of slanderous accusations, men (usually fathers) can be jailed without trial or due process.

By endorsing a feminist policy that is so morally bankrupt, the Morrison government displays a disturbing lack of compassion for the wellbeing of all male victims of domestic violence. Such a policy is based on a discredited feminist approach that perpetuates false assumptions, such as that domestic violence is depicted and seen solely as a male problem and always perpetrated by men against women.

And yet, data keeps mounting which indicates that domestic violence may be perpetrated by both men and women against their domestic partners. Indeed, about a decade ago an official letter by the Harvard Medical School informed that "the problem is often more complicated, and may involve both women and men as perpetrators". Based on the findings of an analysis of more than 11,000 American men and women ages 18 to 28, the letter concluded:

> When the violence is one-sided women were the perpetrators about 70% of the time. Men were more likely to be injured in reciprocally violent relationships (25%) than were women when the violence was one-sided (20%). That means both men and women agreed that men were not more responsible than women for intimate partner violence. The findings cannot be explained by men's being ashamed to admit hitting women, because women agreed with men on this point.[3]

The Harvard Medical School's letter is based on a seminal work published in the prestigious *American Journal of Public Health* (2007).

Written by four leading experts in the field (Daniel J. Whitaker PhD, Tadesses Laileyesus MS, Monica Swahn PhD, and Linda S. Saltman PhD), it seeks to examine the prevalence of reciprocal (i.e., perpetrated by both partners) and non-reciprocal domestic violence, and to determine if reciprocity is related to violence and injury. After analysing data on U.S. adults aged 18 to 28 years, which contained information about domestic violence reported by 11,370 respondents on 18,761 heterosexual relationships, the following conclusions were reached:

- A woman's perpetration of domestic violence is the strongest predictor of her being a victim of partner violence;
- Among relationships with non-reciprocal violence, women were reported to be the perpetrators in a majority of cases;
- Women reported greater perpetration of violence than men did (34.8% vs 11.4 %, respectively).[4]

Professor Linda Mills is the Ellen Goldberg Professor at New York University. She is the principal investigator of studies funded by the National Science Foundation and National Institute of Justice which focus on treatment programs for domestic violence offenders. Her leading studies in the field are published by *Harvard Law Review*, *Princeton University Press, Journal of Experimental Criminology, Cornell Law Review* and other journals. As Professor Mills points out:

> *Years of research, which mainstream feminism has glossed over or ignored, shows that when it comes to intimate abuse, women are far from powerless and seldom, if ever, just victims. Women are not merely passive prisoners of violent intimate dynamics. Like men, women are frequently aggressive in intimate settings and therefore may be more accurately referred to as "women in abusive relationships" (a term I prefer to the more common usages "battered women," "victim," or "survivor")…*
>
> *The studies show not only that women stay in abusive relationships but also that they are intimately engaged in and*

part of the dynamic of abuse. As the studies of lesbian violence demonstrate, women are capable of being as violent as men in intimate relationships. And women can be physically violent as well as emotionally abusive. That violence comes out in their intimate relationships both as resistance and as aggression. We need to put aside our preconceptions of gender socialization and roles.[5]

As early as the 1980s academic researchers such as Dr Murray A. Straus, a professor of sociology at the University of New Hampshire, developed research demonstrating that women are just as likely as men to report physical and emotional abuse of a spouse. These findings have been confirmed by more than 200 studies of intimate violence and they are summed up in Dr Straus's *Thirty Years of Denying the Evidence on Gender Symmetry in Partner Violence.* This article indicates that, despite the common assertion, most of partner violence is mutual and self-defence explains only a small percentage of partner violence by either men or women. Rather than self-defence, 'the most usual motivations for violence by women, like the motivations of men, are coercion, anger, and punishing misbehaviour by their partner'. As noted by Dr Straus:

Pearson (1997) reports that 90% of the women she studied assaulted their partner because they were furious, jealous, or frustrated and not because they tried to defend themselves. These motives are parallel to the motivations of male perpetrators.

Research on homicides by women shows similar results. For example, Jurik and Gregware (1989) studied 24 women-perpetrated homicides and found that 60% had a previous criminal record, 60% had initiated use of physical force, and 21% of the homicides were in response to "prior abuse" or "threat of abuse/death." A larger study by Felson and Messner (1998), drawing upon 2,058 partner homicide cases,

*determined that 46% of the women perpetrators had previously
been abused, but less than 10% had acted in self-defense.*[6]

The Australian Bureau of Statistics Personal Safety Survey
reveals that proportions of non-physical abuse (for example,
emotional abuse) against men have risen dramatically over the last
decade, with 33 per cent of all people who reportedly experienced
violence by a domestic partner being male. And yet, one of the
tactics used by domestic violence campaigners is to highlight only
men's violence and leave out any statistics relating to women.

There is constant pressure to present domestic violence as a
'male problem', and place all the blame for such a violence on men as
a collective group. As a result, and based on a theory that addresses
the problem essentially as a male problem, male victims are often
met with disbelief, even suspicion, when they seek protection from
a violent partner.

In general, domestic violence against male partners are grossly
under-reported, which is partially explained by the fact that men who
sustain this form of violence are unlikely to seek help for these issues
out of a reasonable fear 'they will be ridiculed and experience shame
and embarrassment'. If they do overcome internal psychological
barriers, they still face unfair external institutional barriers in seeking
help from social services and the criminal justice system.

For instance, males seeking help often report that when they
call the police during an incident in which their female partners
have been violent, the police sometimes 'fail to respond or take a
report'. Indeed, male victims of domestic violence encounter greater
animosity when contacting the police. This can be contrasted to
the 'positive and supportive' attitude of police extended to women
who accuse their husbands of violence. According to Dr Sotirios
Sarantakos, who is adjunct professor in the School of Humanities
and Social Sciences at Charles Sturt University:

Most interesting is the finding regarding the practice of women running to the police after hitting the husband, although they hit him without a reason. Even threatening to go to the police was often taken very seriously by the husbands—not without reason.

The positive and supportive attitude of the police and authorities to women's position was reported to have encouraged many wives to take advantage of this and to become even more aggressive at home. Even when they had severely assaulted the husband, their statement that they had been assaulted and abused by him at that time or previously was sufficient for the police to treat them as innocent victims.[7]

This might explain why so many men who sustain violence are deeply reluctant to report their partners. Compared to abused women, there are few social programs or non-profit organisations providing useful assistance to men who are the victims of domestic violence. Instead, male victims often experience external barriers when contacting these social services. When they locate the few resources that are specifically designed to accommodate the needs of male victims, hotline workers often infer that they must be the actual abusers and refer them to batterers' programs.

Within the judicial system, male victims are often treated unfairly solely because of their gender. Indeed, men who make claims of domestic violence face a deeply hostile system, which is far less sympathetic in its treatment of abused men. This is an area in which the "gender paradigm" has caused gross instances of injustice. Indeed, even with apparent corroborating evidence that their female partners were violent to them, male help-seekers often report that they lost child custody as a result of false accusations. As noted by Professor Denise A. Hines (Psychology) and Dr Emily M. Douglas (Social Policy),

Male help-seekers have reported that their complaints concerning their female partners' violence have not always been taken seriously, yet their partner's false accusations have reportedly been given serious weight during the judicial process (Cook 1997). Other men have reported similar experiences in which their female partners misused the legal or social service systems to inappropriately block access between them and their children or to file false allegations with child welfare services (Hines et al 2007).

According to some experts, the burden of proof for IPV [i.e.; intimate partner violence] victimization is high for men because it falls outside of our common understanding of gender roles (Cook, 1997); this can make leaving a violent female partner that much more difficult. For example, many men who sustained IPV report that they stayed with their violent female partners in order to protect the children from their partner's violence. The men worried that if they left their violent wives, the legal system could still grant custody of the children to their wives and that perhaps even their custody rights would be blocked by their wives as a continuation of the controlling behaviors of their wives used during the marriage (McNeely et al, 2001).[8]

The Morrison government has caved in to feminist lobbying. Our Prime Minister is now sponsoring a policy that demonises Australia's men by portraying domestic violence solely in terms of male violence against women. Such a one-sided policy announcement appears to present Australian men as the sole culprits of every instance of domestic violence.

Unfortunately the Labor Party is certainly no better than the Liberals on this issue. On the contrary, we have seen calls from the Prime Minister to "change the hearts of men", and from the Opposition leader, to "change the attitudes of men", as if there were some kind of unspoken bond between these politicians and the men who commit violence against women. As journalist and sexologist Bettina Arndt correctly points out, the Labor Party has made it very clear they intend to push even further in this direction, with endless funds for feminist causes, even more pandering to the activists and ignoring the true issues.

These political leaders see no problem to offend Australian men by assuming that violence against women is an "accepted part" of our society. However, according to Claire Lehmann, editor of *Quillete* magazine, "crimes against women are stigmatised and punished harshly. Sexual offenders generally are given lengthy prison sentences and are secluded from other prisoners precisely because the crime is so reviled — even in prison". In the distorted world of identity politics embraced by the Australian politicians, writes Lehmann:

> [I]ndividuality is subsumed into the collective. When one man holds power, he doesn't do so on behalf of himself, he does so on behalf of the male collective. Likewise, when one man commits a murder, collectivists will portray it as being done in the service of all men. This regressive world view has no qualms about ascribing collective guilt to entire groups of people. But ascribing collective guilt strikes at the very heart of our understanding of justice and liberty.[9]

Clearly, these Australian politicians believe that these anti-male statements will have popular support, particularly from women voters. But judging from the letters received by Bettina Arndt in response to her 2016 an article in *The Australian* about research showing the prominent role women played in violence in the home, there are many in our community, including many women, who are extremely uncomfortable with gender politics. Many of these women have witnessed their sons, brothers, fathers, and male friends experiencing violence at the hands of a woman.

Like ourselves and so many others, they will be deeply disappointed that our Prime Minister has made such a sexist, one-sided policy announcement. It is to the Morrison government's shame that it has signed on to a biased campaign depicting men as the sole agents of domestic violence, most particularly white men and boys. The obscured truth is that women are also violent, but feminist ideologues and their panderers don't want you to know that.

Chapter 14 endnotes

1   Based on: A. Zimmermann, 'The Demonisation of Australian Men', *Quadrant Online*, February 14, 2019, at https://quadrant.org.au/opinion/qed/2019/02/the-demonisation-of-australian-men/. Revised and updated by Prof Augusto Zimmermann and Dr Rocco Loiacono.

2   Stephen Baskerville, *Taken By Custody: The War Against Fathers, Marriage, and The Family* (Nashville/TN: Cumberland House, 2007), 165.

3   'In Brief: Domestic Violence: Not Always One Sided', Harvard Medical School, September 2007, at https://www.health.harvard.edu/newsletter_article/In_Brief_Domestic_violence_Not_always_one_side.

4   Daniel J. Whitaker PhD, Tadesse Haileysus MS, Monica Swahn PhD, and Linda S. Saltzman PhD, 'Differences in Frequency of Violence and Reported Injury between Relationships with Reciprocal and Nonreciprocal Intimate Partner Violence' (2007) 97 (5) *American Journal of Public Health*, pp. 941–47. At the time of this study, Dr Daniel J. Whitaker and Dr Linda S. Saltzman were with the Division of Violence Prevention., National Center for Injury Prevention and Control, Centers for Disease Control and Prevention, Atlanta/GA. Tadesse Haileyesus was with the Office of Statistics and Programming, National Center for Injury Prevention and Control. Manica Swahn was with the Office on Smoking and Health, Center for Disease, Control and Prevention.

5   Linda Mills, *Insult to Injury: Rethinking our Responses to Intimate Abuse* (Princeton University Press, 2003), 8.

6   Murray A. Straus, 'Thirty Years of Denying the Evidence on Gender Symmetry in Partner Violence: Implications for Prevention and Treatment' (2010) *Partner Abuse* 332, 333.

7   Sotirios Sarantakos, 'Deconstructing Self-Defense in Wife-to-Husband Violence', (2004) 12 (3) *The Journal of Men's Studies* 277, 287.

8   Denise A. Hines and Emily M. Douglas, 'Women's Use of Intimate Partner Violence Against Men: Prevalence, Implications and Consequences' 18 (2009) *Journal of Aggression, Maltreatment & Trauma* 572, 573.

9   Claire Lehmann, 'Eurydice Dixon: 'Rape culture' facts just don't fit', *The Australian*, 23 June, 2018, at https://www.theaustralian.com.au/nation/inquirer/eurydice-dixon-rape-culture-facts-just-dont-fit/news-story/fdb16c36d04d48889fb4e181fb98e913.

Part 4

COVID-19

Chapter 15

Scott Morrison: Australia's "Lord Protector"[1]

As legal academics who support the rule of law we have been against the imposition of the draconian measures to fight Covid-19 since they began. We believe they are arbitrary, disproportionate to the threat posed and ultimately a gross violation of fundamental rights.

Here are the undisputed facts about Covid from the Australian Institute of Health and Welfare. The average lifespan of an Australian is 82.6 years. The average age of Covid fatalities in Australia is 85. As at September 2021, the Covid fatality rate for Australians under 50 is four in 12,000. Sixty-six per cent of Covid deaths have been in nursing homes. Seventy-three per cent of Covid deaths involved pre-existing chronic health conditions and a higher number involved non-chronic but somewhat serious health complications.[2]

Politicians have justified the incredible harm they are causing to the Australian people by getting completely drunk on their own sense of self-righteousness. Full of themselves, they proudly warned that we face a great threat but their policies have saved us from the spread of a deadly virus. The privileged members of our political class are able to block our peaceful protests because they think they know better what needs to be done, and even if we are eventually oppressed, silenced and made destitute as a result.

A reasonable concern for the nation's well-being is one thing. However, the actions taken by politicians during this pandemic have gone well beyond the extreme. What is happening is unacceptable and it gives new meaning to the phrase, "a cure worse than the disease". Of course, some of the worst crimes against humanity have been committed by those who believe they are simply doing a "great good". Listening to the patronising remarks of our political rulers brings to mind a famous quote by Christian apologist and novelist C.S. Lewis. In *God in the Dock: Essays on Theology and Ethics*, he stated:

> *Of all tyrannies, a tyranny sincerely exercised for the good of its victims may be the most oppressive... Those who torment us for our own good will torment us without end for they do so with the approval of their own conscience.*[3]

The political philosophy of John Locke is particularly relevant to our understanding of the matter. In the constitutional struggle of parliamentary forces against the Stuart monarchs in 17th Century England, Locke elaborated a theory in which the primary justification for civil government rests on the preservation of inalienable rights to life, liberty and property.

Locke's main concern in his political writings was the elaboration of a legal-political philosophy to underpin the Glorious Revolution of 1688. He developed a distinctly Western political tradition based on the idea that everyone is endowed by God with inalienable rights, and that no government must ever violate these basic rights of the individual.

More importantly, Locke distinguished what is legitimate political power from a situation in which the exercise of power becomes despotic and/or paternalistic. As Locke himself pointed out: "*The great mistakes about government have ... arisen from confounding this distinct power [political power] with another [paternal power]*".[4]

Paternalism is governmental action that limits a person's liberty with the intent of promoting "their own good" regardless of the will of the person. It implies a disregard for the will of a person and involves behaviour that expresses an attitude of superiority. According to emeritus professor of government Geraint Parry, one of the primary purposes in Locke's political theory, "was to separate political power from despotic power and paternal power – in other words, to deny that there is any analogy between the political relationship and the relationships which exist between either masters and slaves or father and children."[5]

The Prime Minister is a typical paternal leader. For example, Morrison has urged his faithful subjects to download a phone app that allows the government to trace our every move. His government was initially aiming for a 40 per cent take up of control of "people's movements and the people they come in contact with". In fact, the app was labelled a complete failure after it failed to help contact tracers identify any people who could be exposed to coronavirus.[6]

While the app that his government developed apparently is voluntary, its introduction raises concerns of such measures becoming more permanent in the future. It also raises privacy issues and concerns that the app could later be used for permanent surveillance. The app presently monitors people's daily interactions using GPS. It uses Bluetooth technology to record contact with other people even if they do not know each other. Although people under 60 have an extremely small chance of dying from coronavirus, Morrison wants to see at least 95 per cent of the population taking the vaccine against such a virus, indeed, initially wanting to make it "as mandatory as you could possibly make it".[7]

Morrison's first instincts are inherently authoritarian and he appears to have developed a visceral distrust of the Australian people.

First of all, what has destroyed our economy is the behaviour of incompetent leaders such as Morrison himself. There were far better and more efficient ways to fight this virus apart from savage bans and gross violations of fundamental rights being inflicted on the people.

Second, the Prime Minister appears to ignore that Australia is a country in which the State has been conceived as deriving from the law and not the law from the State. The Morrison government has no more valid powers than those <u>explicitly</u> granted by the Australian Constitution.

Of course, this is the same government, through then Chief Medical Officer, now Secretary of the Commonwealth Health Department, Brendan Murphy, and then Deputy Chief (now Chief) Medical Officer Paul Kelly, that told us that roughly 150,000 Australians would die from Covid-19, which modelling has been shown to be seriously flawed.[8] It is also the government that unreasonably banned therapeutics such as hydroxychloroquine/zinc, which numerous health experts say "could be our best cure" in the fight against the coronavirus.[9]

It has emerged in the Aged Care Royal Commission that the Morrison government failed miserably at developing policies to protect residents of nursing homes, they being the most vulnerable and where the highest incidence of death from and with Covid-19 has occurred.[10]

What is happening here is nothing short of deeply tragic. Remarkably, Locke famously argued that governments have no other end, "but the preservation of these rights, and therefore can never have a right to destroy, enslave, or designedly to impoverish the subjects".

If a government exceeds the limits of its legitimate power, citizens have the fundamental right to resist. As Locke famously put it in Chapter XIX of his *Second Treatise on Civil Government*:

> *Whenever the legislators endeavour to take away and destroy the rights of the people, or to reduce them to slavery under arbitrary power, they put themselves into a state of war with the people, who are thereupon absolved from any further obedience, and are left to the common refuge which God hath provided for all men against force and violence.*

We should not be too hasty in dismissing Locke's advocacy for fundamental rights and the traditional concept of lawful resistance against political tyranny. This is our constitutional tradition and it firmly communicates not only that some of our rights are inalienable but also that there cannot be one rule for some and another for the rest of us.

Chapter 15 endnotes

1   Based on: A. Zimmermann, 'Prime Minister Scott Morrison, the "Lord Protector" of All Australians', *Caldron Pool*, April 16, 2020, at https://caldronpool.com/prime-minister-scott-morrison-the-lord-protector-of-all-australians/; and A. Zimmermann, 'It's Time to Resist the Paternalistic Behaviour of Australia's Politicians', *The Good Sauce*, October 7, 2020, at https://goodsauce.news/its-time-to-resist-the-paternalistic-oppression-of-australias-politicians/. Revised and updated by Prof Augusto Zimmermann and Dr Rocco Loiacono.

2   For a very detailed outline, see: Luke Massey, 'Just the facts: Coronavirus in Australia by the numbers', *The Spectator Australia*, September 10, 2021, at https://spectator.com.au/2021/09/just-the-facts-coronavirus-in-australia-by-the-numbers/.

3   C. S. Lewis, *God in the Dock: Essays on Theology and Ethics*, Eerdmans Publishing Company, 1970.

4   John Locke, An Essay concerning the true original, extent and end of civil Government (1690), *XV - Of Paternal, Political and Despotical Power Considered Together, 169.*

5   Geraint Parry, 'Individuality, Politics and the Critique of Paternalism in John Locke', (1964) 2 *Political Studies* 1, at 1.

6   Jonathan Kearsley, 'COVIDSafe tracing app labelled a $2 million failure', 9News, July 13, 2020, at https://www.9news.com.au/national/coronavirus-covidsafe-tracing-app-labelled-a-failure-after-not-helping-identify-potentially-exposed-people/2698ebf0-31fd-488f-a4e7-2afbb276a303.

7   Richard Ferguson, 'Future Vaccine Should Be Mandatory, Says PM', *The Australian*, August 19, 2020, at https://www.australian.com.au/nation/coronavirus-australia-live-news-fears-grow-of-sydney-hotel-breach-outbreak/news-story/cf35fb9ae2901600276fa78ee89a2dc5; 'Prime Minister rejects compulsory COVID-19 vaccine', August 19, 2020, at https://www.2gb.com/prime-minister-rejects-compulsory-covid-19-vaccine/.

8   Alan Jones, 'Argue against the alarmism and all you get is vilification', Sky News Australia, October 18, 2021, at https://www.skynews.com.au/opinion/alan-jones/argue-against-the-alarmism-and-all-you-get-is-vilification-alan-jones/video/9ffaacf9d1e219f608dae0fdd86f1bd7.

9   See, inter alia: Dr Harvey A Risch, 'The Key to Defeating COVID-19 Already Exists. We Need to Start Using It', *Newsweek*, August 23, 2020, at https://www.newsweek.com/key-defeating-covid-19-already-exists-we-need-start-using-it-opinion-1519535; Andrew Bolt, 'Potential Coronavirus Treatments Are Being "Patronisingly Dismissed"', *The Bolt Report*, Sky News Australia, August 26, 2020, at https://www.skynews.com.au/details/_6184621840001; Rebecca Weisser, 'No Warp Speed For Aussie Covid Wonder Drug', *The Spectator Australia*, August 8, 2020, at https://www.spectator.com.au/2020/08/no-warp-speed-for-aussie-covid-wonder-drug/.

10 Royal Commission into Aged Care and Safety, *Aged care and COVID-19: A special report*, September 30, 2020, Commonwealth of Australia, p. 11 https://agedcare.royalcommission.gov.au/sites/default/files/2020-10/aged-care-and-covid-19-a-special-report.pdf.

Chapter 16

Morrison: Be Careful Who You Trust for Advice[1]

New Zealand Prime Minister Jacinda Ardern has joined Australia's National Cabinet to contribute to the discussions about the Covid-19 response. Scott Morrison was delighted to invite his New Zealand counterpart to attend the meeting with all Australian states, territory premiers and chief ministers.

Curiously, Morrison suggested to Ardern a similar app to the controversial *COVIDSafe* app be developed for New Zealand. The app, which is used to trace Australian citizens, allows officials to de-encrypt contact information from the user's phone on the basis of a positive Covid-19 result. According to Dr Vanessa Teague, the chief executive of *Thinking CyberSecurity* and an adjunct professor at the Australian National University, the "centralised" tracing app created by the Morrison government "inevitably means the authorities are getting a complete list of your contacts".[2]

Morrison was most likely not interested to discuss how his National Cabinet "ludicrously delayed reopening of the economy to repair the very mess for which it is totally responsible". By entirely trusting the "anointed" advice of carefully selected medical advisers, writes emeritus professor David Flint, Morrison's National Cabinet not just "failed to protect the vulnerable to the high degree necessary", but it "went beyond the pale in imposing a draconian and wholly unnecessary lockdown".[3] By assessing the matter from an essentially constitutional law perspective, Professor Flint concluded:

> *In clear breach of the [Australian] constitution as originally intended, the National Cabinet imposed massive and unprecedented debt on the people, unlawfully suspending and destroying jobs, small business and much of the economic life of the nation as well as grotesquely limiting the people's freedom with something approaching house arrest. The [Australian] people never agreed to this coup, this unconstitutional seizure of power … There was never an emergency which justified the use of such extreme powers.*

As for New Zealand, on March 23, 2020, a month after the country recorded its first case of coronavirus, Prime Minister Ardern announced a draconian national lockdown when it only had 102 cases and zero deaths. While people can argue the NZ government were only trying to stamp out the virus, during this crisis it has been patently obvious that such a lockdown was used to increase the arbitrary power and control of the State over the citizens. "Undoubtedly we now have a tightly-knit oligarchy running New Zealand", writes NZ political commentator Amy Brooke. As noted by her:

> *Initially, most New Zealanders acquiesced to what has been assessed as 'the most significant impact on human rights in living memory', with government imposing lockdown level four. However, the estimated number of deaths of those unable to access hospitals for scheduled cancer, kidney, heart and other urgent surgery and care is apparently going to be far greater than from Covid-19. Reportedly, 20,000 operations and 60,000 specialist appointments have been cancelled. This does not include the mental stress and anxiety of some who may well commit suicide, forced into financial ruin, with business collapsing nationwide, the loss of jobs and savings being eaten away.*

New Zealand had no new cases of coronavirus more than a month after its strict lockdown began. However, over the same period new legislation was hastily passed in the country's Parliament, allowing police to search homes without warrant and ignoring all concerns for basic rights and freedoms of citizens.

Passed by 63 votes to 57, the coronavirus legislation was apparently required for the enforcement of further restrictions, including social distancing and other draconian measures resulting in sweeping police powers. According to that country's Attorney-General, David Parker, the new law had been designed specifically to stop the spread of Covid-19. Mr Parker said the legislation would ensure all the restrictions on gatherings and physical distancing are still fully enforceable.

Chief Human Rights Commissioner, Paul Hunt, was not so impressed. He expressed "deep concerns" about "the lack of scrutiny and rushed process for the Bill". "This is a great failure of our democratic process. The new legislation ... will result in sweeping police powers unseen in this country", he said.

This was not the first time the Prime Minister of New Zealand took advantage of the "pandemic" to use her "extraordinary" powers to introduce legislation devoid of sufficient public consultation. For example, while the population was distracted with dealing with the "pandemic", her government had rushed to introduce "the most extreme abortion law in the world".

Addressing the NZ Parliament on March 25, 2020, to justify the nation going "into an extreme lockdown", Ardern contended that the job of her government and the job of every New Zealander was to save human lives. A State of National Emergency was said to be necessary to preserve such lives. For this particular purpose, she menacingly stated: "There will be no tolerance... We will not hesitate to use our enforcement powers if needed".[4]

Surely the preservation of human life also applies to unwanted new born babies, in particular those who have survived a "failed abortion". Interestingly enough, polling showed prior to the enactment of an Act legalising abortion on demand, women in New Zealand strongly opposed any changes proposed, with only 2 per cent of them supporting abortion being available on-demand up to birth, and 93 per cent opposing sex-selective abortion.

Why did Morrison invite such controversial leader to join Australia's National Cabinet, one who took full advantage of the coronavirus hysteria not only to undermine fundamental rights but also to rush the world's most extreme abortion legislation? Please don't get us wrong. We are quite happy for both leaders to talk about things. However, we would be seriously concerned if the Australian Prime Minister seriously believed that he has anything good to learn from a person who has demonstrated no regard for the fundamental rights of every human being, particularly unwanted babies who are left to die unassisted after a "failed" abortion.

Chapter 16 endnotes

1   Based on A. Zimmermann, 'Scott Morrison: Be Careful Who You Trust for Advice', *The Western Australian Legal Theory Association*, May 18, 2020, at https://walta.net.au/2020/05/18/scott-morrison-be-careful-who-you-trust-for-advice/. Revised and updated by Prof Augusto Zimmermann and Dr Rocco Loiacono.

2   Michael McGowan, 'Privacy Concerns Persist Over Australia's Coronavirus Tracing App', *The Guardian*, April 20, 2020, at https://www.theguardian.com/world/2020/apr/20/privacy-concerns-persist-over-australias-coronavirus-tracing-app.

3   David Flint, 'Professor Lockdown and the Hypocrisy of the Elites', *The Spectator Australia*, May 16, 2020, at https://www.spectator.com.au/2020/05/professor-lockdown-and-the-hypocrisy-of-the-elites/.

4   NZ Herald, 'Your Job is to Save Lives – PM to NZers Ahead of Lockdown', NewstalkZB, March 25, 2020, at https://www.newstalkzb.co.nz/news/national/coronavirus-lockdown-jacinda-ardern-tells-public-your-job-is-to-save-lives/.

Chapter 17

Getting On With the Job? What Job, Precisely, Prime Minister?[1]

On 27 October 2020, the Prime Minister said it was "the right decision" of the Victorian Premier to impose lockdown draconian measures that have been responsible for the greatest violation of fundamental rights in Australia's history in response to a motion moved by opposition leader Anthony Albanese ahead of question time celebrating Victoria's reopening after defeating a second wave of coronavirus infections.

Why is the federal government – and the Prime Minister in particular – so hostile to the exercise of fundamental freedoms?'

In answer to this question, James Allan, the Garrick Professor of Law at the University of Queensland, wrote in *The Australian* that we do not have just a Coalition government that does next to nothing to protect free speech and other fundamental freedoms of the citizen. In fact, he comments, "Prime Minister Scott Morrison has never shown any real interest in free speech and freedom generally. He once remarked sardonically that it didn't create jobs – this from a government that has destroyed more jobs than any other Australian government".[2]

The Morrison government spent a staggering $700 billion last year, with the national debt heading more than one–trillion dollars. In other words, this government is taking taxpayers straight to a one-trillion dollar debt burden; progressing towards a one-and-a-half trillion dollar debt and eventually a two-trillion dollar debt.

This is all done allegedly to protect our jobs, although (at the time of writing) the unemployment rate is now well above 20 per cent in states like Victoria. According to an analysis by the Institute of Public Affairs, over 230,000 small businesses in Victoria are expected to close once Covid-19 measures are finally removed. The closure of these small businesses will permanently destroy 470,000 jobs, based on the average small business employment.

In March 2020 Professor Zimmermann wrote an open letter to Scott Morrison. Published in *Quadrant*, he humbly asked the Prime Minister to reconsider what was happening to the national economy, our civil rights, and to our next generation of Australians. He acknowledged that he was working off the advice of a few health experts but advised him to be careful about group-thinking, and aware that even small wrong decisions could have very bad and unpredictable consequences.

With this in mind the Prime Minister was referred to the comments of Dr John Ioannidis, a professor of medicine, of epidemiology and population health, of biomedical data science, and of statistics at Stanford University in California. When discussing the death rate for Covid-19, Ionnidis authoritatively stated that the official 3.4 per cent rate from the World Health Organisation (WHO) might have caused horror but they were meaningless because the real rate, adjusted from wide age range, could be as low as 0.05 per cent.[3]

Not only did the Prime Minister ignore this advice but his so-called "National Cabinet" entirely accepted the very alarmist and totally inaccurate WHO prediction of 3.4 per cent mortality, and suddenly brought about all these disruptions of personal freedoms that have cost millions of jobs and the closing down of countless businesses. In reality, on 26th October 2020, global cumulative rates were around 43 million and deaths approximately one million – a death rate of 0.02 per cent.

The Prime Minister keeps telling us that his government is simply doing what a panel of scientists is telling them to do. However, there are a number of leading medical practitioners who strongly oppose any measures of social distancing and lockdowns solely on health grounds. For example, hundreds of U.S. physicians composed an authoritative document on May 19, 2021, referring precisely to these health problems, and asking governments to immediately end the coronavirus shutdown.

Although people under 65 have an extremely small chance of dying from coronavirus, the Prime Minister believes that 95 per cent of the population must take the vaccine against such a virus. He initially wanted the vaccine to be as mandatory as possible. 'I expect that it would be mandatory as you can possibly make it', Morrison said, adding that he is 'talking about a pandemic which has destroyed the global economy and taking the lives of ... [hundreds of] Australians'.

Of course, what is effectively undermining our economy is the arrogant and incompetent behaviour of the Prime Minister. There were far better and more efficient ways to fight this virus apart from savage bans and gross violations of constitutional rights. For example, Mr Morrison is presently using his so-called 'cabinet' to ban Australians from leaving their country. He oversees a regime that has shut down international travel, enforcing prohibitions matched only by some of the world's worst totalitarian regimes, notably North Korea and Cuba.

At the time of writing, about 60,000 people have so far been allowed to leave Australia, but approximately 18,000 have not. Numerous other Australians did not even bother to apply since they know their application would be summarily rejected. What is more, according to the Department of Foreign Affairs and Trade ('DFAT'), there are about 20,000 Australians who desire to return but are not being allowed to come back. They are trapped overseas and some effectively running out of money, thus experiencing a desperate situation overseas.

Incidentally, the constitutionality of border control measures in Western Australia have the object of impeding interstate intercourse. These directions attack a basic constitutional right, namely our freedom of movement guaranteed in Section 92 of the Australian Constitution. Enshrined in our Constitution, this basic right is what gave effect to the very concept of Australia as a free, united and independent nation, reflecting in the eyes of our founding fathers one of the primary reasons for the country's very establishment and existence.

In an August 7, 2020 official letter addressed to WA Premier Mark McGowan, the Prime Minister assured him that the Commonwealth would do absolutely nothing to challenge the unconstitutionality of border control measures in Western Australia; that the Coalition government would "immediately and completely withdraw from the proceedings, doing exactly what was asked of it by [the WA Labor government]".

Perhaps even more disturbing is Morrison's refusal to criticise Victoria's Premier Daniel Andrews, in keeping with his strong belief in "national leadership unity". This is despite Victoria's bungled quarantine system, believed to be responsible for the outbreak of community transmission. As stated by Janet Albrechtsen in her column in the *The Australian*, the imposition of stage-four restrictions on Victorians, particularly those living in Melbourne, may lead to far "more people dying", and also to "untold economic harm to millions of Victorians and damaging the economy, a dangerous spike in mental health illnesses especially among young Victorians, and negative educational outcomes".[4]

However, the Prime Minister backed the Victorian Premier, including his imposition of *de facto* martial law. Morrison not only refused to criticise the Premier for being unable to stop the spread of the virus, he further encouraged political arbitrariness in Victoria by, in his own words, "encouraging the Victorian government to ensure that there are appropriate penalties for those who do break public health notices." Surely we should expect the leader of a Liberal government to be interested in protecting personal freedoms, not suppressing them. Yet we get this spineless guff instead: "Daniel Andrews has my full support … I will give him every support he needs".[5] Offering such enthusiastic support to the authoritarian measures of the Victorian government is actually "the only thing that matters".[6]

Granted, the Liberal governments in New South Wales, South Australia and Tasmania have also been far too willing to rule by decree and impose their own arbitrary measures on citizens. But the fact that the federal government constantly endorses violations of fundamental rights should not come as a surprise for those who have read the Institute of Public Affairs's *Legal Rights Audit 2019*.

The report's main author, Morgan Begg, first explains that "fundamental legal rights are necessary to achieve justice within a legal system and act as a vital constraint on the coercive power of the state". However, he claims these legal rights have been breached by 381 separate provisions in Acts of Australia's Federal Parliament. As Begg points out, "The Coalition is trashing fundamental legal rights of all Australians, creating an unprecedented challenge to individual freedom and human dignity," writes Begg, a research fellow with the Institute of Public Affairs.[7]

Sir Robert Menzies would be appalled to see what has become of the party he founded. Menzies believed that the progress of our nation depended not so much upon the security provided by the State, but upon personal freedom. In a keynote speech delivered on January 21, 1943, ironically about the founding principles of Liberal Party, Menzies compared then free and democratic societies such as Australia, to dictatorships such as Nazi Germany. Why then, asked

Menzies rhetorically, would the Allies eventually defeat them at war? His answer was patently clear:

> *We shall defeat them by proving once more that a free individual living in a free community with a free tomorrow in front of him (or her) is worth a nation of slaves.*

Perhaps most disturbing is to observe how the Australian people, and Victorians in particular, appear to have developed a servile mindset and blind faith in government. In a free society, argued Menzies, there is an innate sense of distrust of government and a healthy appreciation of our basic rights and responsibilities which confer upon every citizen a certain measure of human dignity by making them effective contributors to the life of the nation. Hence, in a well-known Melbourne address to his fellow Victorians, on September 7, 1947, Menzies declared:

> *If we fought for freedom, and as we fought for it, did we secure it? Are we pursuing paths along which we will eventually end up by finding ourselves bond, or free? Why was it that in 1939 we said that the Germans were not free?... It consisted in that the German people, in return for that mess of pottage, had handed over to a few men their birthright and said to a few men: "You rule us, you govern us, you order us.*

What Menzies was asking of his Victorian audience back then is precisely what we should be asking now. "When we have the all-powerful state," Menzies argued, "the people will then be the servants of that state and the minds of those people will be servile minds, because there will only be only one master – the state inhuman but all-powerful!"

This is the challenge Victorians now face under their Labor government. Australians at large face a similar challenge under a federal government dominated by a party that has become "liberal" in name only. Premier Andrews may be a ruthless political ruler, but the Prime Minister has tacitly endorsed the undermining of the rule of law and oppression of the people in that particular State. To be sure, according to Janet Albrechtsen, "few expected Morrison would criticise hefty restrictions on fundamental rights in Victoria. He has admitted publicly that these matters are of little interest to him."[8]

When will the Prime Minister stop compromising the future of our nation as a free and prosperous nation? As noted by Dr Paul Collits, "Morrison and Andrews need one another. While Andrews exists, Morrison escapes even the merest modicum of scrutiny. While Morrison exists, with his "national cabinet", Andrews gets protection".[9]

Chapter 17 endnotes

1   Based on: A Zimmermann, 'Getting on with the Job? What Job, Precisely, Prime Minister?', *The Spectator Australia*, November 1, 2020, at https://www.spectator.com.au/2020/11/getting-on-with-the-job-what-job-precisely-prime-minister/ and A. Zimmermann, 'Australia, How Have You Let it Come to This?, *Quadrant Online*, August 12, 2021, at https://quadrant.org.au/opinion/qed/2020/08/australia-how-have-you-let-it-come-to-this/. Revised and updated by Prof Augusto Zimmermann and Dr Rocco Loiacono.

2   James Allan, 'Academic Peers Gag Their Own, Amid Alarming Signs On Free Gag In Tasmania', *The Australian*, October 26, 2020, at https://www.theaustralian.com.au/commentary/academic-peers-gag-their-own/news-story/475d6d206de04be3c8b36ecfd45fe79e.

3   See: John P A Ioannidis, Infection fatality rate of COVID-19 inferred from seroprevalence data, October 14, 2020, at https://www.who.int/bulletin/volumes/99/1/20-265892.pdf.

4   Janet Albrechtsen, 'PM Monsters A Patsy But Indulges A Villain', *The Australian*, October 27, 2020, at https://www.theaustralian.com.au/commentary/scott-morrison-monsters-australia-post-boss-christine-holgate-but-indulges-daniel-andrews/news-story/c72a025ac8513a065f7f2c54879a1fcc.

5   Heath Parkes-Hupton, 'Scott Morrison Urges Australians to Support Victoria Through Critical New Lockdown Measures, *The Australian*, August 3, 2020, at https://www.theaustralian.com.au/breaking-news/scott-morrison-urges-australians-to-support-victoria-through-critical-new-lockdown-measures/news-story/a7a62eab55ef290185ed06d72a4d9720.

6   Natalie Oliveri, 'PM Says Victoria's Premier Has His Full Support to Tackle State's Coronavirus Crisis', Today Channel 9, at https://9now.nine.com.au/today/ coronavirus-australia-scott-morrison-says-daniel-andrews-has-full-support-victoria/ fd460c9a-db46-408f-82d2-a6e82ef3b865.

7   Morgan Begg and Kristen Pereira, 'Legal Rights Audit 2019', Institute of Public Affairs, February 2020, p 1. As Mr Begg points out in his excellent Legal Rights Audit, the federal Liberal governments have been directly responsible for at least 279 fundamental legal rights breaches since 1976, compared with only 102 breaches under Labor. This is the equivalent to 11 breaches for each year of Liberal government compared with 5 breaches each year on average under Labor. – See also: Morgan Begg, 'Coalition Government Trashes Legal Rights', *IPA Today*, February 7, 2020, at https://ipa.org. au/publications-ipa/media-releases/coalition-government-trashes-legal-rights   See also: Nicola Berkovic, 'Coalition Worse than ALP on Human Rights', *The Australian*, February 6, 2020, at https://www.theaustralian.com.au/business/legal-affairs/ coalition-worse-than-alp-on-human-rights/news-story/0bc3d71cd4daf8ab425f3bd5 d8edba11.

8   Janet Albrechtsen, 'PM Monsters A Patsy But Indulges A Villain', *The Australian*, October 27, 2020, at https://www.theaustralian.com.au/commentary/scott-morrison-monsters-australia-post-boss-christine-holgate-but-indulges-daniel-andrews/news-story/c72a025ac8513a065f7f2c54879a1fcc.

9   Paul Collits, 'When We Needed Churchill – We Got ScoMo', The Freedoms Project, September 16, 2020, at https://www.thefreedomsproject.com/item/567-when-we-needed-churchill-we-got-scomo.

Chapter 18

The Prime Minister's Failure to Uphold the Constitution[1]

In a letter dated August 7, 2020, the Prime Minister communicated to Premier Mark McGowan that the Commonwealth would do absolutely nothing to challenge the border-control measures imposed in Western Australia. Rather, Scott Morrison informed that his government will 'immediately and completely withdraw from the procaeedings, doing exactly what was asked of it by the Western Australian government'. In the event of the High Court eventually seeking a view of his government about this matter, the Prime Minister assured the WA Premier that the Commonwealth would 'positively support [the government of] Western Australia in any way it could outside the courtroom, having withdrawn from the proceedings at [the government of] Western Australia's request'.[2]

Sources from the government admitted the Commonwealth's withdrawal from the case meant the Court was able to 'dodge the question of the validity of the border closure directions'. The then Attorney General Christian Porter actually confessed that removing the Commonwealth from this constitutional matter before the High Court was "unusual" but the Morrison Government had "listened to the WA government's concerns". "We acted on Western Australia's request (not to intervene), and prioritised the need to work cooperatively with them during the pandemic",[3] he said. Working cooperatively with the state government to undermine constitutional rights and freedoms, in other words.

This is simply appalling and says a lot about our politicians' commitment to uphold the Constitution. As a consequence, the High Court decided in November 2020 that Clive Palmer's challenge to Western Australia's border closure had failed. The five judges who heard this challenge produced four judgments that run to a total of 105 pages. The Court accepted that the Western Australian government could close the state's borders on grounds that it did so based on a proportionality test. At paragraph 80 of the joint judgement, Chief Justice Susan Kiefel and Justice Patrick Keane stated:

> ... the defendant's submission that there is no effective alternative to a general restriction on entry must be accepted.[4]

The facts involving the case read as follows. On March 15, 2020, the Government of Western Australia declared a state of emergency on grounds of a "pandemic". On November 6, the High Court answered questions referred to in a case concerning whether the two pieces of legislation authorising the draconian measure, the *Quarantine (Closing the Border) Directions* (WA) ('Directions') and the authorising *Emergency Management Act 2005* (WA) (the Act), were constitutionally invalid. The plaintiffs sought a declaration of invalidity because the Australian Constitution, in section 92, provides that "trade, commerce and intercourse among the States ... shall be absolutely free".

Section 56 of the Act empowers the Minister for Emergency Services to declare a state of emergency provided he is satisfied of the occurrence of an emergency and that extraordinary measures are required to minimise the "loss of life, prejudice to the safety, or harm to the health, of persons". Section 67 relevantly empowers an authorised officer "for the purpose of emergency management" during a state of emergency, to direct or prohibit the movement of persons into an emergency area. The closure of state borders were issued pursuant to paragraphs 4 and 5 of the Directions, thus prohibiting as from April 5, 2020 the entry of any person into Western Australia unless authorised by the State government ("subject of exemption").

The closure of the state borders effectively violated section 92 of the Australian Constitution. The combined effect of these two laws unconstitutionally prohibited cross-border movement to Western Australia. Not only have they imposed a direct burden on the freedom of intercourse, but also a discriminatory burden with a naturally protectionist effect and, as a consequence, contravenes the freedom of trade and commerce also protected under the relevant constitutional provisions.

However, on February 24, 2021, in the case of *Palmer v Western Australia*, the High Court unanimously and in separate judgments discovered that the provisions of the Act authorising the Directions were actually "valid". Although it accepted that section 67 of the Act effectively imposes a substantial burden on interstate intercourse, by reference to the purpose of the provisions on the declaration of a state of emergency and the making of directions, the Court found that the burden was justified and the provisions "did not infringe the constitutional limitation in s 92".

Section 92 of the Constitution informs that any interstate trade, commerce, and intercourse "shall be absolutely free". According to Chief Justice Kiefel and Justice Keane, such a guarantee of absolute freedom: "is not really absolute' and it should 'not be taken literally". Instead, they assumed the validity of laws which affect interstate trade, commerce and intercourse but whose purpose is allegedly not of a protectionist kind. In doing so, they argued that section 92 is concerned primarily "with freedom from unjustified burdens of a discriminatory kind".

Anstey Wynes's *Legislative, Executive and Judicial Powers in Australia* (1956) is broadly recognised as a classic treatise on the distribution of legislative, executive and judicial powers of the

Commonwealth and the States under the Australian Constitution. Published in 1936, the first edition of this work "was rightly welcomed ... as the first book of substance in the Australian constitutional field for some time". A book review of its fifth edition published in the *Federal Law Review* describes this important book as 'the principal modern text and modern reference book for those concerned with what may loosely be called the 'Lawyer's Constitution'.[5]

We are only referring to this because Dr Wynes in his seminal book comments that '[t]he freedom prescribed in section 92 is not limited to freedom from legislative action, nor is sec. 92 limited in its application to the States'. He goes on to remind us that, under the best rules of constitutional interpretation, the 'absolute freedom' prescribed in section 92 'is not limited in its operation to discriminatory laws, although any legislation or executive action discriminating against inter-State trade, commerce and intercourse, would be clearly invalid'. This certainly contradicts the opinion of the Court that section 92 is primarily 'concerned with freedom from unjust burdens of a discriminatory kind'. Although it is undoubtedly true that a state law which discriminates against interstate, as opposed to intrastate, intercourse would be clearly invalid, the absence of discriminatory provisions does not make such law a valid one. Indeed, the freedom of movement explicitly prescribed in section 92 is absolute and certainly not limited to 'unjustified burdens of a discriminatory kind'.[6]

It appears to us, writing as two legal academics, that the intent of the Constitution has been grossly misrepresented. We are astounded to see how a judge may find the words conveyed in section 92 "unclear". Of course, the words in section 92 are extremely clear. They effectively mean what it says: that any trade, commerce and intercourse among the States shall be absolutely free. It is rather elementary to conclude that the drafter intended that these things should be absolutely free of any governmental restrictions whatsoever. The reason section 92 does not refer to specifics is simply because it was not intended to be specific. It is meant to be a broader statement that any restriction, including the protection of persons from an alleged pandemic, is unconstitutional.

Of course, it is difficult to accept that these judges sincerely believe there was no other effective alternative to these draconian border restrictions. Professor Anthony Gray "respectfully" and "fundamentally" disagrees with this understanding. In an excellent article for the *Western Australian Jurist,* he convincingly argues that the idea of freedom of trade, commerce and intercourse within Australia was "absolutely fundamental to the creation of the nation and its foundations legal document".

As Professor Gray reminds us, in a Constitution that is largely barren of express rights protection, section 92 is 'a standout example'. 'The vision of a unified, connected nation is clearly evident. It must be maintained', he argues. Apart from the elementary fact that there were far more reasonable and effective ways to protect the safety of citizens during the Covid-19 "health crisis", the purpose of having a written constitution "is to place certain values about the day to day exigencies". According to Gray,

> *There were a multitude of other options available to the WA government short of the hard lockdown. They could have applied the border closure to Victoria alone, they could have insisted on a fourteen-day quarantine, they could have insisted that people have a COVID test before crossing the border.*[7]

It is as if the Western Australian government believes that Australia is "merely a collection of self-governing fiefdoms, not a unified nation". When one reads the origins of section 92, it is patently clear that it was all about making Australia a united nation. The great "Father of the Australian Federation", Sir Henry Parkes, would be totally appalled to see the Constitution he helped develop being so completely distorted. The reformulation of section 92 entirely contradicts the vision of Parkes, who stated at the First Australasian Convention, in 1891:

> Australia shall be free – free on the borders, free everywhere – in its trade and intercourse between its own people; that there shall be no impediment of any kind – that there shall be no barrier of any kind between one section of the Australian people and another; but that the trade and the general communication of these people shall flow on from one end of the continent to the other, with no one to stay its progress or to call it to account... [8]

Sir Henry Parkes died in 1896, before the last two federal conventions. However, at the Adelaide Convention Debates, in 1897, the original draft previously supported by him was basically left unchanged. There was only a minor change in the draft clause, which referred to trade "throughout the Commonwealth" and not "among the States". It was suggested that "among the States" was better a phrase than the broad phrase "throughout the Commonwealth". The final result is the present provision to be found in section 92, which provides:

> On the imposition of uniform duties of customs, trade, commerce, and intercourse among the States, whether by means of internal carriage or ocean navigation, shall be absolutely free.

As can be seen, the statement in section 92 is crystal clear and it entirely dispels any possible doubt about its effective meaning. John Quick and Robert Garran further elaborated upon all possible implications of the relevant provision. Quick played a prominent role in the Federation movement and the drafting of the Australian Constitution. As for Garran, throughout the 1890s he was deeply active in the Federation movement as one of Sir Edmund Barton's assistants, as a councillor of the Australasian Federation League of New South Wales, and as an organiser of the unofficial conferences supporting Federation at Corowa (1893) and Bathurst (1896).

When it comes to an understanding of the original meaning of section 92, surely there is no better source than Quick and Garran's seminal *The Annotated Constitution of the Australian Commonwealth*. First published in 1901, in this authoritative commentary on the Australian Constitution, these celebrated authors elucidated the authentic meaning or purpose of section 92. According to them, an important question needs to be considered in connection with section 92 in order to grasp its full significance: What is absolute freedom of trade, commerce and intercourse? In reference to this question, Quick and Garran replied authoritatively:

> *Absolute freedom of trade, commerce and intercourse may be defined as the right to introduce good, wares, and merchandise from one State into another, the right to sell the same, and <u>the right [of citizens] to travel unburdened by State restrictions, regulations, or obstructions</u>.*[9]

Section 92 is written in relatively simple language to describe a basic concept that any trade, commerce and intercourse among the States shall be "absolutely free". This is certainly not vague but the Western Australian government has chosen to violate the constitutional provision and the High Court has failed in its duty to uphold the Australian Constitution.

When one reads the authentic meaning conveyed in the explicit words of section 92, it is patently clear that the drafters desired to put this in simple English language so that no lawyer could ever misinterpret it. Of course, this has not stopped the High Court from ignoring the constitutional provision to the extent that these judges accepting the deeply controversial argument posed by the Western Australian government that there were no alternatives to the draconian closure of its State borders.

This is simply appalling and it says a lot about the character of our politicians. The Constitution says in its Preamble that we 'have agreed to unite in one indissoluble Federal Commonwealth'.

However, it is now quite obvious that the intent of the Founding Fathers has been ignored by our political establishment with the endorsement of an unelected judicial elite. The High Court should uphold the challenge and we could then hold a popular referendum – direct democracy – that would allow the people to decide whether any amendments to the Constitution might be necessary.

This is not about Mr Palmer but whether we are still a united nation or not. Right now we are not. In bowing to WA Premier Mark McGowan's wish that the Commonwealth withdraw from Clive Palmer's bid to reopen the state's borders, the Prime Minister stands condemned for an appalling dereliction of duty to uphold the Constitution. That left the High Court to ignore history and the clear meaning of words in a decision that would have sickened the Founding Fathers.

Chapter 18 endnotes

1   Based on: A. Zimmermann, 'How the High Court Redefined 'Absolutely'', *Quadrant Online*, March 4, 2021, at https://quadrant.org.au/opinion/qed/2021/03/how-the-high-court-redefined-absolutely/. Revised and updated by Prof Augusto Zimmermann and Dr Rocco Loiacono.

2   Prime Minister Scott Morrison, 'Letter to The Hon Mark McGowan MLA, Premier of Western Australia' (August 7, 2020).

3   Rosie Lewis, 'Clive Palmer loses WA border bid in High Court', *The Australian*, November 6, 2020, at https://www.theaustralian.com.au/nation/clive-palmer-loses-wa-border-bid-in-high-court/news-story/c56244b064dc5cf9a41dbc2e563aa754.

4   *Palmer v The State of Western Australia* [2021] HCA 5 [80] (Kiefel CJ and Keane J).

5   P. Brazil, 'Review of Legislative, Executive and Judicial Powers in Australia by W. Anstey Wynes LLD of the South Australian Bar (1977)' (1977) 8(3) *Federal Law Review* 371.

6   W. Anstey Wynes LL.D., *Legislative, Executive and Judicial Powers in Australia* (2nd ed., The Law Book Co. of Australia, 1956), 390.

7   Anthony Gray, 'Covid-19 Border Restrictions and Section 92' (*The Western Australian Jurist*, Volume11 / Connor Court, 2020) 135.

8   Quoted in Chris Merritt, 'High Court Ruling on Clive Palmer's Border Challenge is a Step In the Right Direction', *The Australian*, February 26, 2021, at https://www.theaustralian.com.au/business/legal-affairs/high-court-ruling-on-clive-palmers-border-challenge-is-a-step-in-the-right-direction/news-story/2b1f344ab1194d1a2a5eec0da859a8ae.

9   Conv. Deb. Adel, 875-7. Cited in John Quick LLD and Robert Randolph Garran MA, *The Annotated Constitution of the Australian Commonwealth* [1901] (LexisNexis, 2002 reprint), 844.

The Andrews Government's Chief Enabler[1]

Victorians have today (June 9, 2021) been promised parole from their locked-down homes and lives, with the second week of the two-tier restrictions — one set of edicts for Melbourne, a slightly more relaxed code for the regions — soon to be amended. This means that Melburnians will be able to leave their homes for other than the five government-ordained reasons that have made prisoners of citizens.[2]

Not that there is all that much to celebrate. Where travel from home is now restricted to 10km, as of midnight on 10 June it will be permissible to venture a whole 25km from your front door. As *Quadrant Online*'s editor tells me, that is still not quite far enough for him to visit, legally, a gravely ill friend, but he will just have to cop it. Like so many of the fines and restrictions imposed over the past 15 months on what used to be normal life, there is little rhyme or reason, and never an explanation, for whatever Spring Street's controlling whims might be on any given day.[3]

In this context, religious services are said to provide hope and comfort in the midst of despair, especially in times of sickness and death. However, going to church has not been considered "essential" by the Victorian government.[4] Gatherings for worship, prayer groups, or other religious purposes were forbidden as "non-essential" activities.

In Melbourne, a pastor has been arrested for defying these draconian measures. Rev Paul Furlong, of Revival Church in the outer suburb of Narre Warren, had already been arrested for daring to post a Facebook video announcing that his church would hold a Sunday service. Victoria was in a seven day lockdown at the time. On Sunday, May 31, 2021, police stormed the outdoor service and ordered his congregation to leave, before issuing infringement notices, wrestling congregants to the ground and arresting Furlong. That outrage is just one of so many that Victoria has seen over the course of the last year and a half.

Rev Furlong was arrested, jailed and refused bail. He is an active evangelist, with a successful ministry that reaches out to many nations, including Pakistan, Kenya, Nepal and India.[5] In a Facebook video, he stated:

> My church is open. I've said I would not shut the church again. This Sunday at 10 am, my church … [is] open for worship… This comes down to a freedom of religion, movement, association.[6]

I wholeheartedly agree with him. If bottle shops are open, which they are and doing a roaring business as Victorians seek respite from isolation in alcohol, then attending religious services definitely should be open too. The freedom to join with fellow worshippers is essential to people of faith. It is scandalous that an Australian government says it is not.

Rev Furlong has had the courage and conviction to resist these oppressive rules — and perhaps his defiance and the price he is paying for it have had an effect, as the latest, updated restrictions are lifting church attendance from 10 people to 75. I think it cowardly of Victorian church leaders to accept the Andrews government's decree that worship is not an "essential service". They should resist these acts of governmental oppression, ensuring that their fundamental freedoms are properly respected. Critical among these are freedom of religion, freedom of speech and freedom of association.

But while the men and women of the cloth disappoint in shrinking from defying the state and its VicPol enforcers, my disappointment is more pronounced in the case of one prominent Christian leader in particular. I speak of Prime Minister Scott Morrison. While his fellow believers in Victoria see their most basic rights violated, Mr Morrison simply refuses to criticise the Andrews government in the name of supporting "national leadership unity". This forbearance is extended despite Victoria's bungled quarantine system which has been directly responsible for each of the state's four-and-counting ruinous lockdowns. Few Victorians, I am told, believe there won't be a fifth.

Yet from Canberra support for Andrews & Co flows unrestrained. Speaking for the Morrison government, Health Minister Greg Hunt declared:

> We think that the Victoria response is fair and appropriate and acknowledge and thank them for that.[7]

At a May 30, 2021 press conference, Hunt also stated:

> We believe that the steps taken by Victoria … are appropriate. And we welcome them.[8]

In a similar vein, the Prime Minister says he has offered the unconditional assistance of the federal government for whatever the Victorian government might need:

> Right now, every support has been given to the Victorian government … and I have made it very clear to the Premier that any other additional support he requires he will receive.[9]

Sadly, Mr Morrison was as good as his word, last week announcing yet another temporary Covid disaster bailout to make possible the latest Victorian lockdown. Need it be said that such support provides further incentive and encouragement for the continuation of these arbitrary measures?[10]

More than $45 billion in federal money has been poured directly into Victoria to support the lockdowns and attempts to ameliorate the consequent damage to industry, the economy and people's lives. Of course, without the financial support of the federal government none of these measures by the state government would be possible.

The Prime Minister often argues that lockdown measures in Victoria are based on "expert health advice", which is the line Victoria's leaders also spout. Yet media requests to see the arguments for lockdowns are rejected out of hand. The little people of Victoria must do as they are ordered, it seems, but have no right to examine the purported reasons why. And yet, as Janet Albrechtsen points out in *The Australian*, such lockdown restrictions, particularly on those living in Melbourne, have led to "untold economic harm to millions of Victorians and damaging the economy, a dangerous spike in mental health illnesses especially among young Victorians, and negative educational outcomes".[11]

Meanwhile, the Prime Minister not only refuses to criticise the Victorian government, he commends it "for their efforts over the last few days". In his own words, he has been "encouraging the Victorian government to ensure there are appropriate penalties for those who do break public health notices".[12]

To give a better idea of what it means in practice, we have witnessed Victoria Police arresting people who dare to promote social media protests against these lockdowns. In September 2020, police in Victoria made international headlines by arbitrarily arresting a pregnant mother in front of her little children in their Ballarat home. She was arrested and charged under section 321 of the *Victorian Crimes Act* 1958, which makes it an offence to "pursue a course of conduct which will involve the commission of an offence". Her "crime": posting a Facebook message announcing there would be a protest against lockdowns in the regional town. The protest would have abided by mask and social distancing requirements, unlike the BLM protest held in June 2020 in Melbourne, to which the Victoria Police conveniently turned a blind eye.

There are questions whether this concerned mother had committed *any* offence under that specific Act, given the lack of intentionality required by the criminal law. There was no element of intentionality in her behaviour, since she was entirely unaware of any illegality. Besides, her Facebook post certainly did not incite people to protest in a manner that was inconsistent with the Stage 3 lockdown conditions then prevailing. To my mind this is an irrefutable violation of fundamental rights in Victoria's *Charter of Human Rights and Responsibilities* but also the constitutional right to freedom of political communication. The Victoria Charter explicitly guarantees to every person their fundamental legal rights to privacy and peaceful assembly as well as freedom of association, movement, thought, conscience, and expression (Sections 12 to 16).

However, Victoria's Police Commissioner Luke Cornelius was "satisfied" that police officers had acted "properly" and "reasonably". He actually accused the concerned mother of engaging in "serious criminal activity", warning that police officers would be deployed to make similar arrests. He then issued the following threat to those who dare to resist any such acts of political tyranny:

> We are very concerned, and in fact, outraged is probably a fair word, to say there are still people in our community who think it's a good idea … to leave home and protest on our streets … Take the selfish option and leave home to protest, we'll be there for you.[13]

How can our system of representative government be reconciled with police bursting into private homes to arrest a mother in front of her children because of a Facebook message? Under the Victorian government, writes Greg Sheridan, "all the mechanisms of democratic accountability have virtually disappeared … Victoria has become a dysfunctional one-party state with a mostly compliant local media".[14]

The arrest of citizens for speaking out is an undeniable mark of every dictatorial regime. However, Premier Andrews has described these police actions as merely "operational matters for Victoria Police". This attitude — that the state is the master of its people, not the other way around — may help to explain his enthusiastic support for the Chinese Communist Party (CCP), which has now been found responsible for the outbreak and spread of the coronavirus that has infected more than 173 million people across the globe.

In a June 7, 2020 article in *The Australian*, Dr Steven Quay, who holds both a master's and a doctorate degree from the University of Michigan, and Richard Muller, an emeritus professor of physics at the University of California-Berkeley, informed readers that Covid-19 is a million-to-one proposition to have arisen naturally. Instead, they believe it extremely likely the virus was created in a CPP lab at the Wuhan Institute of Virology. And yet, "Daniel Andrews is standing firm on China", writes political report Richard Willingham for the *ABC News*. Amidst all this, offering full support to Premier Andrews and his authoritarian regime, is the Prime Minister. Surely he should be deeply concerned about all these violations of human rights. Instead, we get this from him:

> Andrews has my full support ... I will give him every support he needs.[15]

As noted by Dr Paul Collits, Morrison and Andrews need each other. "While Andrews exists, Morrison escapes even the merest modicum of scrutiny. While Morrison exists, with his national cabinet, Andrews gets protection".[16]

Premier Andrews is an authoritarian ruler, no doubt about it, and the Prime Minister is effectively empowering and facilitating his arbitrary government. Indeed, the Morrison Government is actively financing and assisting these draconian, lockdown measures that have inflicted great pain and suffering to the people of Victoria.

Chapter 19 endnotes

1   Based on A. Zimmermann, 'The Andrews Government's Chief Enabler', *Quadrant Online*, June 9, 2021, at https://quadrant.org.au/opinion/qed/2021/06/the-andrews-governments-chief-enabler/. Revised and updated by Prof Augusto Zimmermann and Dr Rocco Loiacono.

2   Melissa Iairia, 'Christian Pastor Arrested for Flouting Lockdown Rules', *The Australian*, May 31, 2021, at https://www.theaustralian.com.au/breaking-news/christian-pastorarrested-for-flouting-lockdown-rules/news-story/3a32aca0908b0c4e86be57c0 de9452bb.

3   'Victoria Extends State of Emergency Powers Enabling Lockdowns Until July 1', *The Australian*, June 5, 2021, at https://www.theaustralian.com.au/breaking-news/victoriaextends-state-of-emergency-powers-enabling-lockdowns-until-july-1/news-st ory/8eec8784545cbb7095cb745253992c63.

4   Mark Powell, 'In a Mental Health Crisis Church Controls Don't Pass the Pub Test', *The Spectator Australia*, May 27, 2020, at https://www.spectator.com.au/2020/05/in-amental-health-crisis-church-controls-dont-pass-the-pub-test/.

5   John Sandeman, 'Pastor on Remand After Church Defies Victoria's Lockdown', *Eternity News*, June 1, 2021, at https://www.eternitynews.com.au/australia/pastor-on-remand-after-church-defies-victorias-lockdown/.

6   Melissa Iairia, 'Christian Pastor Arrested for Flouting Lockdown Rules', *News.Com.Au*, May 31, 2021, at https://www.news.com.au/national/victoria/courts-law/christian-pastor-arrested-for-flouting-lockdown-rules/news-story/3a32aca0908b0c4e86be57c 0de9452bb.

7   Josh Butler, 'Morrison Defends Victoria Response', *The New Daily*, May 31, 2021, at https://thenewdaily.com.au/news/2021/05/31/victoria-lockdown-morrison/.

8   The Hon Greg Hunt MP, 'Press Conference in Canberra with a COVID-19 Vaccine Rollout Update, Outbreak in Australia and Federal Government Support for Victoria', Commonwealth Government, Department of Health, May 31, 2021, at https://www.health.gov.au/ministers/the-hon-greg-hunt-mp/media/press-conference-incanberra-with-a-covid-19-vaccine-rollout-update-outbreak-in-australia-and-federalgovernment-support-for-victoria.

9   'Federal Government Announces Help for Victoria As It Enters COVID Lockdown', May 27, 2021, at https://www.abc.net.au/news/2021-05-27/federal-governmentvictoria-help-covid-outbreak-lockdown/100170310.

10 'Temporary COVID Disaster Payments Will Begin Next Week as Part of Victorian Government Support', 7 News, June 4, 2021, at https://7news.com.au/business/finance/500-covid-payments-set-to-begin-for-victorians-within-days-as-national-cabinet-decides-funding-c-3010603. See also: Georgia Hitch, 'Greater Melbourne Workers Affected by COVID Lockdown Eligible for Commonwealth Payments', ABC News, June 3, 2021, at https://sydneynewstoday.com/500- temporary-covid-disasterpayments-will-begin-next-week-as-part-of-victoriangovernment-support/213482/.

11 Janet Albrechtsen, 'She Won't Talk, She Tweets – Pericles Would Wince', *The Australian*, August 11, 2020, at https://www.theaustralian.com.au/commentary/she-wont-talk-shetweets-pericles-would-wince/news-story/44919481b8d7da08c923b96 bb8b027e0.

12 Heath Parkes-Hupton, 'Scott Morrison Urges Australians to Support Victoria Through Critical New Lockdown Measures, *The Australian*, August 3, 2020, at https:// www.theaustralian.com.au/breaking-news/scott-morrison-urges-australiansto-support-victoria-through-critical-new-lockdown-measures/news-story/ a7a62eab55ef290185ed06d72a4d9720.

13 Naaman Zhou, 'Victorian Bar Criticises Arrest of Pregnant Woman for Facebook Lockdown Protests Post as Disproportionate', *The Guardian*, September 3, 2020, at https://www.theguardian.com/australia-news/2020/sep/03/victoria-police-arrestedpregnant-woman-facebook-post-zoe-buhler-australia-warn-lockdown-protesters.

14 Greg Sheridan, 'Daniel Andrews' leadership is superficial and a failure', *The Australian*, August 6, 2020, at https://www.theaustralian.com.au/commentary/daniel-andrewscleverly-leads-in-a-vacuum-of-democracy/news-story/075dce1f0b2dda2c69 3077e92e3ac467.

15 Natalie Oliveri, 'PM Says Victoria's Premier Has His Full Support to Tackle State's Coronavirus Crisis', *Today Channel 9*, June 25, 2021, at https://9now.nine.com.au/ today/coronavirus-australia-scott-morrison-says-daniel-andrews-has-full-support-victoria/fd460c9a-db46-408f-82d2-a6e82ef3b865.

16 Paul Collits, 'When We Needed Churchill – We Got ScoMo', The Freedoms Project, September 16, 2020, at https://www.thefreedomsproject.com/item/567-when-we-needed-churchill-we-got-scomo.

Chapter 20

Why the Prime Minister Must Be Held Accountable for the Australian States' Human Rights Violations[1]

The Premier of Western Australia has recently ordered 75 per cent of WA's workforce to get vaccinated or face job losses or a possible $20,000 fine. Mark McGowan has also decided that he won't be opening the State borders to unvaccinated people.

A major objective seems to be the preparation of the citizen for a docile surrender of all their fundamental rights, always in the name of an overly protective, benevolent State. In the name of the "health" of the people, politicians can now happily implement the most unthinkable and atrocious perversities.

In the midst of such human rights violations, there is also the tacit support of the Prime Minister. Not only has Scott Morrison been tacitly supporting these arbitrary measures, but also objectively misleading the population by claiming that the Federal Government has no ability to 'override' these State laws and executive orders.

The rise and growth of international law has increased the size and significance of Australia's external affairs. The principle that the external affairs power now extends to allow the federal government to regulate any matters related to the protection of fundamental rights is commonly accepted by the courts.

The Australian Constitution, in its Section 51 (xxix), says:

> *The Parliament shall, subject to this Constitution, have power to make laws for the peace, order, and good government of the Commonwealth with respect to… (xxix) external affairs*

The phrase 'external affairs' refers to persons, places, matters, or things geographically external to Australia. It enables the federal Parliament to pass any law concerning topics related to the protection of human rights, including the prohibition of compulsory vaccination.

The federal Executive can enter into international agreements as part of its general executive power under s 61. To become part of domestic law, treaties must be enacted by Parliament under s51 (xxix).

The rise and growth of international law has dramatically increased the significance of the external affairs power. As the range of topics regulated under s 51(xxix) has been gradually expanded, federal legislation has more often come into conflict with State legislation.

Accordingly, a federal law will be valid even on the basis of formal dealings of the federal Executive, which then could legislate on fundamental rights and protections for the Australian citizen.[2]

Sir Harry Gibbs, a former Australian Chief Justice, in a well-known academic article explained that, together with the regular operation of s. 109 (inconsistency) of the Constitution, the external affairs power has the potential to 'annihilate State legislative power in virtually every respect'. Gibbs concluded:

> *It appears no exaggeration to say that the combined effect of s 51(xxix) and s 109 is that the Commonwealth can annihilate State legislative power in virtually every respect.*

Section 109 of the Constitution provides that federal laws must prevail over those of a State to the extent of any inconsistency. The State law is then deemed invalid to the extent of the inconsistency.

Situations of conflict between a State law and a federal law may arise, for example, when:

> *a) the State law cannot be obeyed at the same time as the federal law (Mabo v Queensland (1988) 166 CLR 186);*
>
> *b) when the federal law permits a certain activity prohibited by a State law (Colvin v Bradley Bros Pty Ltd (1943) 68 CLR 151);*
>
> *c) when a federal law confers a right which a State law seeks to remove (Clyde Engineering Co Ltd v Cowburn (1926) 37 CLR 466).*

The Australian government has entered into thousands of treaties on a wide range of matters. In *R v Burgess; Ex parte Henry* (1936), the Court ruled that the external affairs power is not restricted to the Commonwealth's power to make laws with respect to the external aspects of the subjects mentioned in s. 51. According to law professors Andrew Stewart and George Williams:

> *Since the Tasmanian Dam Case (1983) the High Court has accepted that this power can be used to pass laws that implement obligations that have been assumed by the federal government under international instruments like treaties and conventions... Given that Australia, as at December 2005, had entered into 2544 international instruments, the possible uses of the external affairs power remain enormous. The fact that it can be used to legislate in areas formerly under State control is, according to the long-accepted approach of the High Court, irrelevant.*[3]

In the Preamble of the World Health Organisation's Constitution, the word "health" is conceptualised as a "state of complete physical, mental and social well-being and not merely the absence of disease or infirmity".

However, to allegedly defeat an apparently deadly virus, draconian measures have caused millions of people to endure highly stressful and traumatic situations, including home confinement, job losses, financial ruin, and a whole host of mental illnesses and challenges. These measures are unlawful not only in accordance with our system of democratic parliamentary government but also under international law. They unlawfully affect the enjoyment of our fundamental rights and freedoms, including freedom of speech, association, movement, expression, and privacy.

"Seriously, one more comment about human rights ... it's about human life", complained Daniel Andrews, the Victorian Premier, about journalists who dare to question the impact on human rights of lockdown measures.[4] For Mr Andrews, "health" not only trumps human rights but shows that the right thing is doing what might be advantageous to the preservation of public health.

International law recognises that, during extraordinary circumstances, the States may enact emergency powers that suspend ordinary rule-of-law protections, with the exception however of "non-derogable rights". The inalienability of certain rights has been acknowledged by the *Siracusa Principles on the Limitation and Derogation Provisions in the International Covenant on Civil and Political Rights* ('Siracusa Principles'). A document produced by the *American Association for the International Commission of Jurists*, the Siracusa Principles, declares that:

> No state party shall, even in time of emergency threatening the life of the nation, derogate from the Covenant's guarantees of the right to life; freedom from torture, cruel, inhuman or degrading treatment or punishment, and from medical or scientific experimentation without free consent; freedom from slavery or involuntary servitude ... the right to recognition as a person before the law; and freedom of thought, conscience and religion. These rights are not derogable under any conditions even for the asserted purpose of preserving the life of the nation.[5]

Australian governments are now starting to impose vaccination mandates as a way out of lockdowns. These governments communicate that the unvaccinated will be treated differently to the vaccinated, some even losing their jobs if they do not comply with the vaccination requirement. In practice, this means that unvaccinated individuals will have less freedom to get a job, to travel and to get together with their loved ones, and to go to coffee shops and restaurants.

This governmental approach creates a two-tier society that is unsupported by the *Nuremberg Code* – an ethics code – relied upon during the Nazi doctors' trials in Nuremberg in 1947. This Code has as its first principle the willingness and informed consent by the individual to receive medical treatment or to participate in an experiment.

Informed consent can be described as the voluntary agreement by an individual to a proposed medical or pharmaceutical treatment, given after sufficient and appropriate information about potential risks and benefits, including possible adverse effects, how common they are, and what they should do about them.

From the perspective of international law, the right to informed consent is the bedrock principle of ethical standards in medicine. According to Article 6(1) of UNESCO's *Universal Declaration on Bioethics and Human Rights* (2005):

> *Any preventive, diagnostic and therapeutic medical intervention is only to be carried out with the prior, free and informed consent of the person concerned, based on adequate information. The consent should, where appropriate, be express and may be withdrawn by the person concerned at any time and for any reason without disadvantage or prejudice.*

As can be seen, international instruments prohibit the removal of non-derogable rights even in situations of an alleged "emergency", including the right to informed consent when it comes to vaccination. This prohibition encompasses any form of compulsion subjecting individuals to mandatory medical or pharmaceutical service, including vaccination.

For any government either by itself or via corporate proxy to attempt to mandate vaccines in circumstances where there has not been adequate testing and analysis of risks as well as benefits would constitute not only a violation of the principle of informed consent, but also a violation of Australia's obligations under international law with respect to medical experimentation.

While the *International Covenant on Economic, Social and Cultural Rights (ICESCR)*, contains no definition of health, the United Nations' *Committee on Economic Social and Cultural Rights* communicates that the right to health contains both fundamental freedoms and entitlements. These freedoms include 'the right to control one's health and body', and 'the right to be free from interference [...] non-consensual medical treatment and experimentation'.

Under article 2(1) of the ICESCR, Australia is legally obliged to take steps 'to the maximum of its available resources, with a view to achieving progressively the full realisation' of the fundamental rights recognised in the Convention.

Article 2(1) of the ICESCR states:

> 1. *Each State Party to the present Covenant undertakes to take steps, individually and through international assistance and co-operation, especially economic and technical, to the maximum of its available resources, with a view to achieving progressively the full realization of the rights recognized in the present Covenant by all appropriate means, including particularly the adoption of legislative measures.*

The United Nations' *Committee on Economic Social and Cultural Rights* has determined that Article 2 (1) 'must be read in the light of the overall objective of the Covenant which is to establish clear obligations for States parties in respect of the full realization of the rights in question'.

This provision, 'thus imposes an obligation to move as expeditiously and effectively as possible towards that goal'. Furthermore, in its Article 4, the ICESCR declares:

> *The States Parties to the present Covenant recognize that, in the enjoyment of those right provided by the State in conformity with the present Covenant, the State may subject such rights only to such limitations as are determined by law only in so far as this may be compatible with the nature of these rights and solely for the purpose of promoting the general welfare in a democratic society.*

The United Nations' *Committee on Economic Social and Cultural Rights* emphasises that the Covenant's limitation clause to be found in Article 4, 'is primarily intended to protect the rights of individuals rather than to permit the imposition of limitations by States'. As also noted by the Committee, 'issues of public health are sometimes used by States as grounds for limiting the exercise of other fundamental rights'.

As a consequence, any State, which, for example, restricts the movement of, or incarcerates, persons with transmissible diseases, refuses to allow doctors to treat persons believed to be opposed to a government, is acting in a manner that is 'incompatible with the nature of the rights protected by the ICESCR'.

In addition, Article 12.2. of the ICESCR acknowledges that the right to health embraces a wide range of fundamental rights which allows people to have a healthy life, such as employment rights and freedoms to movement and association.

Yet, these fundamental freedoms are being profoundly undermined in Australia. The Australian government is directly in conflict with these freedoms.

In George Orwell's dystopian novel, *Nineteen-eighty four*, the 'New Thought Police' were able to control the ideas that determined the political and cultural values of society. The withdrawal of personal freedoms was sold in Australia as a positive thing. Slavery to the State was presented as the gateway to freedom and prosperity.

The Morrison government had the ability to override State laws which violate fundamental rights and freedoms. However, the Prime Minister claims there is nothing his government can do. This is certainly not so and one does not need to be a prophet to predict that dark days will descend upon Australia.

Some crimes are committed by commission and others by omission. The Morrison government is surely guilty of the latter.

Chapter 20 endnotes

1   Based on: A. Zimmermann, 'Can Canberra Be Held Accountable Internationally For Human Rights Abuses From State Lockdown Laws', *The Spectator Australia*, November 2, 2021, at https://www.spectator.com.au/2021/11/can-canberra-be-held-accountable-internationallyfor-human-rights-abuses-from-state-lockdown-laws/. Revised and updated by Prof Augusto Zimmermann and Dr Rocco Loiacono.

2   "The first thing to be stressed about s 51(xxix) of the Constitution for the purposes of the present case is that its reference to "external affairs" is unqualified. The paragraph does not refer to "Australia's external affairs". Nor does it limit the subject matter of the grant of power to external affairs which have some special connection with Australia. The words "external" means "outside". As a matter of language, it carries no implication beyond that of location. The word "affairs" has a wide and indefinite meaning. It is appropriate to refer to relations, matters or things. Used without qualification or limitation, the phrase "external affairs" is appropriate, in a constitutional grant of legislative power, encompass both relationships and things: relationships with or between foreign States and foreign or international organizations or other entities; matters or things which are territorially external to Australia regardless of whether they have some identified connection with Australia or whether they be the subject matter of international treaties, dealings, rights or obligations. Such a construction of the phrase "external affairs" in s 51(xxix) is supported by the settled principle of constitutional construction which requires that, subject to any express or implied general constitutional limitations and any overriding restrictions flowing from express or implied constitutional guarantees, the grants of legislative power contained in s 51 be (sic) construed with all the generality which the words used admit and be given their full force and effect". – *Polyukhovich v The Commonwealth* (the War Crimes case) (1991) 172 CLR 501 [599] (Deane J.)

3   Andrew Stewart and George Williams, *Work Choices: What the High Court Said* (Sydney/NSW: Federation Press, 2007), 10.

4   Janine Graham, 'The Informer: 'Seriously, One More Comment About Human Rights…', Says Daniel Andrews', *The Canberra Times*, July 27, 2020, at https://www.canberratimes.com.au/story/6851881/seriously-one-more-comment-about-human-rights/.

5   United Nations Economic and Social Council, United Nations Sub-Commission on Prevention of Discrimination and Protection of Minorities, Siracusa Principles on the Limitation and Derogation of Provisions in the International Covenant on Civil and Political Rights, Annex, UN Doc E/CN.4/ (1984), [58].

CONCLUSION

Scott Morrison: The Hollow Man

In a piece published in *The Spectator Australia* on October 28, 2020,[1] Rocco Loiacono referred to Scott Morrison as 'a hollow man'. This was inspired by a poem studied at high school, T.S. Eliot's *The Hollow Men*, published in 1925.[2] It deals with the otherworldly journey of the spiritually dead, who fail to transform their motions into actions, conception to creation, desire to fulfilment. The first lines of the poem are these:

> *We are the hollow men*
> *We are the stuffed men*
> *Leaning together*
> *Headpiece filled with straw. Alas!*
> *Our dried voices, when*
> *We whisper together*
> *Are quiet and meaningless*
> *As wind in dry grass*
> *Or rats' feet over broken glass*
> *In our dry cellar.*

Several literary critics[3] note the regret of these 'hollow men' regarding their sterility and lack of conviction in their lives. In previous chapters we have elaborated on Scott Morrison's sterility and lack of conviction as a leader of a centre-right, conservative party. In the piece we referred to above we focussed in particular on the situation in Victoria and the Prime Minister going out of his way to praise the Victorian Premier, Daniel Andrews, for his heavy-handed approach, in the interests of "national unity". We were not alone. *The Australian's* Janet Albrechtsen had plenty to say on the matter, contrasting Morrison's meekness towards Andrews with his confected outrage directed at Christine Holgate, the former Chief Executive of Australia Post. Holgate's 'crime' was to hand out four Cartier watches, valued at $20,000, to senior executives as rewards for a $66m deal with big banks over banking arrangements. Morrison bellowed in parliament that he was "shocked and appalled", demanding Holgate stand aside and "if she doesn't wish to do that, she can go!"[4] Albrechtsen wrote:[5]

> *If the Prime Minister wants to discard Labor's cartoon sketch of him as Scotty from Marketing, he might start by showing more consistency when he employs outrage for political effect. Victorians, and others, might wonder why he didn't muster up the same killer political instinct towards the Victorian Premier, whose lockdown cost the country $100m a day in lost GDP, 1200 jobs lost every single day, and $200m a day in support from taxpayers across the country.*
>
> *Contrast the PM's mostly supine approach to Andrews over many months. To be sure, few expected Morrison would criticise hefty restrictions on fundamental human rights in Victoria. He has admitted publicly that these matters are of little interest to him. Still, it has been bewildering that Morrison has not been at the frontline to hold Andrews to account for incompetence that has killed more than 700 Australians and a lockdown that has caused so much further damage.*
>
> *Morrison should get to know Victorians better. They need a federal leader who will hold Andrews to account for damage done. Indeed, it's high time the Liberal Party, state and federal,*

stopped treating Victoria like a protected "progressive" species
that leans naturally left, to be handled with kid gloves.

Contrast Morrison with Liberal leaders like John Howard and Tony Abbott, who stood out for their conviction. For most of his public life, Howard affirmed how he was inspired by Reagan and Thatcher's conservatism. Their success in government centred on the implementation of core conservative ideals: lower taxes, smaller government, reward for individual effort, defence of the family and the importance of: national sovereignty, the rule of law and, above all, individual liberty.

Howard's conviction to fight for these conservative ideals was not always convenient for him, especially during his time as Opposition Leader in the 1980s, when Mr Howard not only had Bob Hawke as an adversary, but many within his own party. He had to contend with constant leaking and undermining by his colleagues and the "beauty contest" polls at the time showed the results of this appalling disloyalty. Some may recall the front-page headline of the now-defunct *Bulletin* on 20 December 1988: "Mr 18%. Why on earth does this man bother?"

However, determined in his view that "it is better to be right than popular", and despite being disgracefully dumped by his colleagues as leader in 1989 (and then rejected in 1990, 1993 and 1994 after the Peacock loss and Hewson fiasco), Howard never wavered from articulating policies that embodied the abovementioned conservative ideals. This determination led him to become Australia's second-longest serving prime minister after Sir Robert Menzies.

Menzies believed that the progress of this country depended more on personal freedom rather than security provided by the State. He outlined this as one of the founding principles of the Liberal Party. In the well-known "Melbourne Address" of 7 September 1947, Menzies declared:

If we fought for freedom, and as we fought for it, did we secure it? Are we pursuing paths along which we will eventually end up by finding ourselves bond, or free? Why was it that in 1939 we said that the Germans were not free?[...] It consisted in that the German people, in return for that mess of pottage, had handed over to a few men their birthright and said: "You rule us, you govern us, you order us".

In 1964, Reagan delivered his famous discourse entitled *A Time for Choosing*, where he outlined the importance of individual liberty:

This is the issue [...] whether we believe in our capacity for self-government or whether we abandon the American Revolution and confess that a little intellectual elite in a far-distant capital can plan our lives for us better than we can plan them ourselves.

Indeed, in his 1981 Inauguration Address, President Reagan declared: "In this present crisis, government is not the solution to our problem; government is the problem."

Upon becoming Conservative Party leader in 1975, Thatcher outlined her vision of a free society:

A man's right to work [...] to spend what he earns, to own property, to have the State as servant and not as master [...] They are the essence of a free economy. And on that freedom all our other freedoms depend.

Throughout her prime ministership, Thatcher held steadfast to this vision. Criticised by weak-kneed colleagues who implored her to make a 'U-turn' on free-market policies, she told them at the 1980 Party Conference: "You turn if you want to. The Lady's not for turning". In defence of individual freedom and the rule of law, she took on and defeated militant unions. In making cuts to profligate government spending, she reminded Britons that the socialists will eventually run out of other people's money. Thatcher warned Britain repeatedly of the dangers of the distant Brussels elite having too much power and the threat this posed to democracy. Some 26 years after she left office, Britons realised Thatcher was right and voted to leave the EU. Her and Reagan's resoluteness in the face of the Soviet Union's aggression led to the fall of the Berlin Wall in 1989.

At the coming federal election, the Coalition Government will be seeking a fourth term in office. At that point in its life cycle, a government seeking re-election would be able to point to its record as justification to the voters that it deserves another go. Unfortunately, this supposedly centre-right government has not enacted a single major reform that its constituency can be proud of. Not one. Mr Morrison in particular appears to be doing everything in his power to disavow core conservative values, with disastrous effects.

A Centre for Independent Studies paper on the response of Australian governments to coronavirus published on December 9, 2020 found that they ignored their own advice, instead whipping up fear with incoherent and unjustified restrictions. In *Victims of Failure – how the COVID-19 policy response let down Australians*,[6] Monica Wilkie argues that governments did not analyse trade-offs that included soaring public debt, unemployment and mental health problems.

"Measures for fighting coronavirus must be justified and proportionate, and individual liberty must always be protected; these are the very standards governments set themselves in their pandemic influenza plans," states Wilkie, noting that principles of good governance and democracy have been ignored.

Indeed, Wilkie asserts that, "by adopting a strategy of coercion early in the pandemic, it became difficult, almost impossible, for responses to the outbreak to abandon this pattern."[7] This can be seen in his rush to embrace, and encourage state premiers to embrace, vaccine mandates and passports. As many commentators, including myself, have pointed out repeatedly in numerous forums, these measure infringe the principle of informed consent to medical treatment, a principle enshrined in the *Australian Immunisation Handbook*, which states clearly that: "[Vaccines] must be given voluntarily in the absence of undue pressure, coercion or manipulation."

On this issue, as with so many others, Morrison's inconsistency is acute.

During a press conference on July 22, 2021,[8] the Prime Minister was asked a question regarding the matter of informed consent to medical treatment:

> *JOURNALIST: Just coming back on that question, just to clarify, can you get informed consent by simply seeing your pharmacist as opposed to seeing the GP? And secondly, can you, can you talk about the two people who sadly died taking AstraZeneca? And would you be worried if one of those people, as I understand it, had, or the family claims, didn't get or wasn't fully informed of the symptoms to look out for.*
>
> *PRIME MINISTER: Well, we're all responsible for our own health. And, when it comes to informed consent and getting consent to whatever treatment or procedure you may have or I may have, then I'm ultimately responsible for what people do in their health treatment to me. And, there has been the opportunity for people to visit their GP to have that consultation. The Government has provided that and funded that, and the informed consent process provides the decision to the individual. That's the sort of country we live in. People make their own decisions about their own health and their own bodies. That's why we don't have mandatory vaccination in relation to the general population here, because people make their own decisions and we encourage people to make those decisions. We make as much information available to them as is*

possible. The vaccines, like any vaccine, with any vaccine, there are risks associated, and I won't go into each of the individual ones because I don't want to particularly draw attention to anyone. But, we all understand that with any vaccine there are risk factors and they're enumerated and they're made available to people, and people make decisions about that.

A year previously, Morrison stated that he respects the views of those who wish to refuse abortion-tainted vaccines,[9] following concerns raised by the Catholic Archbishop of Sydney, Anthony Fisher, and Anglican Archbishop Glenn Davies. They raised serious ethical and moral considerations for their flock regarding the production and testing of coronavirus vaccines with the cell lines of an electively aborted foetus.[10] The senior Sydney clerics sought assurances it would not be mandatory and nobody would be forced to prescribe or dispense it. They also urged the prime minister to ensure an "ethically uncontroversial alternative" would be made available.

However, despite previous promises to the contrary, at the time of writing, Morrison, his government and state premiers seem determined to steamroll Australians every day towards medical Jim Crow,[11] where unvaccinated people will be considered unclean and thus unfit to participate in society. In fact, Morrison, his government and state premiers seem determined to gaslight the public, labelling those who are unvaccinated as "a threat to public health". This is despite increasing evidence from around the world demonstrating that any benefit conferred by the vaccine is entirely personal, which benefit may not be that great.

However, the Prime Minister's first instincts are always inherently authoritarian. He appears to have developed a visceral distrust in the Australian people. We are supposedly living in a free society and it is quite extraordinary that the Prime Minister attempts to coerce citizens to do something they might not want to do.

Australia is a country in which the state has been conceived as deriving from the law and not the law from the State. Since this is a document of limited powers, the Morrison government has no more powers than those explicitly granted by the Constitution. Whereas Section 51 (xxiiiA) of the Australian Constitution allows for the granting of various services by the federal government, this should not be to the extent of authorising any form of civil conscription. In other words, no Australian government, or those acting on its behalf, is constitutionally authorised to make the Australian people take any medicament against their best will.

Instead of using the full power of the state to command his "subjects" to do whatever they might want, Mr Morrison still needs to learn that true democratic leaders use the power of persuasion and rational argument in order to convince their fellow citizens to do what is right.

We know for sure that vaccinated people can still catch and transmit the virus, including from each other. This was confirmed by Professor Andrew Pollard, who led the Oxford vaccine team, to a British Parliamentary Committee.[12] This is why, at the time of writing, the British Government has decided not to introduce vaccine passports[13] and will repeal some of the emergency powers under its *Coronavirus Act 2020*.[14] As pointed out by numerous Tory backbenchers – Coalition MPs, take note – vaccine passports are a redundant measure in light of ongoing community transmission and serve only to increase distrust of governments, and thus serve no good point. And if there is no point, then they are an infringement on basic human rights. No ifs, no buts.

Mr Morrison has acquiesced in the trampling of fundamental rights and freedoms by consistently supporting state government imposed lockdowns. As noted above, his support of Daniel Andrews was particularly contemptible, telling the Federal Parliament that it was the "right decision of the Victorian Premier" to impose the draconian lockdown measures. His egregious silence following the arrest of Zoe Buhler, a pregnant woman in her pyjamas, in her own home, for daring to question these measures on social media speaks volumes. This attitude is consistent with Mr Morrison's past statements on his lack of belief in the importance of free speech in a thriving liberal democracy.

In this regard we must go back to March 2017, when Mr Morrison was Treasurer in the Turnbull Government. At this time, attempts were being made to amend section 18C of the Commonwealth *Racial Discrimination Act* 1975, which prohibits an act that is reasonably likely to "offend, insult, humiliate or intimidate" someone because of their race or ethnicity. It had been Coalition policy to either repeal this law or amend it significantly, since it infringes the implied right in the Australian Constitution of freedom of political communication given that the language and emotions 18C targets – offence, insult and humiliation – go far beyond what is required in the international treaties most directly supporting this Act, they being the *International Covenant on Civil and Political Rights* (ICCPR) and the *International Convention on the Elimination of All Forms of Racial Discrimination* (ICERD).

During the debate on the legislation to amend the Act, Mr Morrison told *The Sydney Morning Herald* on March 1, 2017 that changing section 18C would not help reduce unemployment or improve any other economic metric. He said at the time: "As a senior figure in this government ... I know this issue doesn't create one job, doesn't open one business, doesn't give anyone one extra hour. It doesn't make housing more affordable or energy more affordable. I don't see any intersection between that issue and those priorities."[15]

Morrison fails to realise that by giving in to cancel culture and wokeness and not tackling the issue of freedom of speech at universities, jobs are actually lost. Peter Ridd had to fight all the way to the High Court for pointing out deficiencies in research on the supposed "bleaching" of the Great Barrier Reef. Neither has this Coalition Government done anything to rein in SBS and the ABC, both unrelentingly hostile to anyone who doesn't agree with their Green-left view of the world. As Chris Kenny wrote:

> *[T]he ABC [..] is less interested in facts than it is in ideology, so that it instinctively is willing to overlook reality because it has a preoccupation with potential partisan motives. Despite its vast resources and expansive staff, no reporter or analyst at the ABC predicted that Scott Morrison was a plausible prospect in 2019.*

> *Getting issues wrong, sometimes disastrously so, is the high price our public broadcaster pays for feeble leadership that allows ideological positions to develop and embed themselves in the organisation. In recent times the ABC has been terribly wrong on those crucial elections but also on Cardinal George Pell and former attorney-general Christian Porter – vendetta journalism has run ahead of the facts.* [16]

When he is not staying silent on these matters, Mr Morrison resorts to glib statements to try to get himself out of trouble, which must be a tactic he honed in his marketing career. In his new year's message to the nation, the Prime Minister had plenty to say about national unity and how actions speak louder than words. He repeated his 'one and free' refrain on Australia Day 2021, a unilateral change to the national anthem which, to use the Prime Minister's own words, 'doesn't create a single job', but has all the hallmarks of placating the mob. He has fallen prey to insidious identity politics, grovelling to appease it by supporting female quotas. The Prime Minister could do worse than to heed Peta Credlin's advice on this matter:

> *He's not sure whether moving Ministers Reynolds and Porter will provide the circuit-breaker he needs. So he's casting around and thinking: 'what about quotas? What says I'm more pro-*

women than that?'. Hear me on this, you don't improve the
Liberal Party by making it more like the Labor Party.[17]

Credlin added that when the Liberal Party is taken closer to the Labor Party, normally it dismays its own best supporters "without gaining any new ones". In this vein Tony Abbot cites Sir Robert Menzies' oft-cited reflection: "We took the name 'Liberal' because we were determined to be a progressive party, willing to make experiments, in no sense reactionary but believing in the individual, his rights, and his enterprise and rejecting the socialist panacea" is sometimes used to make conservatives look like interlopers in the party he formed.[18] However, to demonstrate the inaccuracy of this assertion, Abbott also refers Menzies' much less familiar despairing 1974 observation in a letter to his daughter Heather about the party's Victorian state executive: "dominated by what they now call 'Liberals with a small l' – that is to say Liberals who believe in nothing but who still believe in anything if they think it worth a few votes. The whole thing is tragic".[19]

The Coalition Government under Scott Morrison seems to have forgotten about the rule of law, and in particular, the Constitution and the principle underpinning it: *one dissoluble Commonwealth.* Rather than defend it, as true conservatives should, along with the Liberal Party's main constituency, small businesses, on his orders the Commonwealth withdrew from Clive Palmer's High Court action against the WA State Government. This is despite academics such as Professor George Williams, who could be considered more to the left of the political spectrum, opining that Commonwealth has various options that could be explored to override the States on borders, be it through the Biosecurity legislation or possibly under the External Affairs power, to guarantee freedom of movement of citizens.[20]

As Janet Albrechtsen wrote in *The Australian* on October 27, 2020:

*Australians might reasonably expect Morrison to test an issue
of major national significance for its constitutional implications.
Shutting state borders will become an unfortunate precedent for
the future. And, as day follows night, the threshold for doing
so again will get lower and lower. It won't be a once-in-a-
generation pandemic that leads to borders closing next time. In
other words, a functioning federation is at stake.*[21]

Further, Professor James Allan noted the jurisprudential
implications of this weakness:

*And don't tell me the s.92 High Court borders case (another
poor effort from our top justices) would have had the same
outcome even if the feds had stayed involved. Leaving it all
to Palmer made it easy for our High Court. If the federal
government doesn't care about borders why should the seven
top judges?*[22]

Further, who could forget Mr Morrison distancing himself from
comments by Treasurer Josh Frydenburg, who stated that he drew
inspiration for economic reform from the legacy of Reagan and
Thatcher.[23] The Prime Minister's response was a vacuous "uniquely
Australian plan"[24] for economic recovery. To this end, it's hard to
imagine that the words "structural reform" will pass the lips of Scott
Morrison or Josh Frydenberg – let alone Simon Birmingham, the
ridiculously unsuitable Finance Minister – any time soon.

Yet Australia is still ranked poorly in terms of its tax structure
among OECD countries.[25] What is more, Australia's personal and
corporate tax rates are among the highest among OECD member
countries.[26] Relative to the OECD average, the tax structure in
Australia is characterised by substantially higher revenues from
taxes on personal income, profits, and higher revenues from taxes
on corporate income and gains; payroll taxes; and property taxes.
In fact, Australia's corporate tax take ranks alongside those of the
highest collecting nations in the developed world.[27] The distortions

and disincentives this creates should be priorities for government, particularly when recovering from a recession.

Australia also has an over-reliance on personal income tax over consumption taxes – almost half at 41%. Analysis of single workers at the income level of the average wage shows Australians pay 23.6 per cent of wage earnings to government in income tax. The OECD average on income tax paid in 2019 was 15.8 per cent. A report commissioned by the New South Wales government in 2020, led by former deputy prime minister, John Anderson, found that Australia's consumption tax is the second-lowest revenue raiser of the advanced economies, forcing governments to rely on damaging taxes on personal income and business.[28]

Additionally, as noted by Tony Makin, the negative economic repercussions of the virus-related budget deficits will play out for a long time and act as a drag on economic growth. Makin points out that, "consistent with numerous studies on the impact of a rise in public debt on growth, the more than 20 per cent rise in its federal public debt to GDP ratio from 2018-19 to 2023-24 could shave 0.5 per cent off annual economic growth in future." The consequences of this debt will have to be faced up to in the coming years, especially as interest rates inevitably rise, since repaying it "soaks up funds that could be used for more productive purposes, further limiting the economic welfare of future generations."[29] In other words, as John Howard showed, once you reduce the budget deficit you can also reduce the tax burden, particularly on the engine room of the economy, small business (yes, those quiet Australians).

Not only has the Coalition failed on fiscal responsibility, which has always been a key tenet of centre-right politics, but also in another area of policy of crucial importance to its small business base, namely, industrial relations reform.

The proposed changes announced to the *Fair Work Act* in 2020 amounted to little more than tinkering at the edges of a system that has been largely responsible for the collapse of enterprise bargaining and low wage growth. The Government failed spectacularly to get even these modest changes through the Senate. Maybe because it didn't really believe in them. Here again, the Morrison Government did its best to distance itself from conservatism, stating in relation to its proposed modest changes that "this is not 1996".[30] No kidding. One of the first major pieces of reform that the Howard Government undertook was in the area of industrial relations, via the *Workplace Relations Act* 1996 (which was law within nine (9) months – that's right, nine (9) months) of John Howard taking office) and laid the groundwork for the fall in unemployment and growth in real wages in the succeeding decade. Prime Ministers had courage (and not in the Sir Humphrey Appleby sense) back then. Menzies would be appalled at what his Liberal Party has become. It no longer advocates for the "forgotten class - the middle class who, properly regarded, represent the backbone of this country [...] taken for granted by each political party in turn".

At the 2019 election, many conservatives went back to the Liberals, given that Malcolm Turnbull had finally been dispensed with, and recalling that Scott Morrison stopped the boats and was a regular churchgoer. What is more, they were genuinely concerned about then Opposition Leader Bill Shorten's 'drastic climate action', handing Morrison a 'miracle' victory in what was called the 'climate change election'. Indeed, in 2019, Morrison said of the ALP's climate change policy that it was "a reckless target ... (that) will come at a tremendous cost to Australians". How can something be so wrong then but now be absolutely right?[31] As noted by Peta Credlin, such a move is a slap in the face to the Coalition's base that voted against 'drastic climate action'. Indeed, Steven Hamilton noted in the *Australian Financial Review* that "a full 80% of remaining emissions reduction is expected to happen purely by technological advancements. As if by magic."[32] As Credlin points out, tellingly:

"Australia is being asked to jeopardise affordable and reliable fossil-fuel-based power now in the hope something will be developed to replace it sometime in the future, demanding a leap into the dark. This is economically irresponsible but politically it's also almost bewilderingly stupid."[33] At the same time, Morrison ruled out nuclear, the only zero emissions baseload technology that there is out there, which Credlin stated was "so wrong-headed",[34] adding that Morrison has "blurred the lines" between the Liberal and the Labor parties with his commitment to net zero by 2050. "They are so similar, other than Tony Abbott stopping the boats back in 2013, what is the difference between these two parties?

"When people go to the ballot box that thought they were voting for a conservative party last time round they will look very, very carefully this time round."[35] As Charles Pier wrote in *The Spectator Australia*:

> [T]he Coalition's brand new climate stand is just like pissing in a wetsuit. It might make them feel nice and warm, but that's about it.

True, there's a crude political calculation in it all. The government is fixing a hole in the roof; a hole which in this case lets voters out rather than rain in.[36]

As we have seen in these pages, Scott Morrison is anything but a conservative.

Should the Coalition lose the upcoming election, Scott Morrison will have no-one to blame but himself. The unfortunate reality is that if you don't always stand on points of principle and fight for values – such as the presumption of innocence or the importance of individual responsibility – when you have the leeway to do so, then you won't get the opportunity to when you don't. As our longest serving Prime Minister, Sir Robert Menzies, said prophetically in a 1946 radio broadcast, "The Choice":

> We need constantly to remind ourselves that democracy
> can produce tyranny just as readily as any other system of
> government unless the individual democrat has learned to
> attach supreme importance to individual freedom.

When you look at its record, the Morrison government is like
Seinfeld, a show about nothing (but without the laughs). It hasn't
achieved anything of significance in three terms that you would
expect a centre-right government worthy of the term to achieve.
Why would it achieve anything in a fourth?

Conclusion endnotes

1   Rocco Loiacono, 'Scott Morrison: dismal with Daniel Andrews, feeble on freedom',
    The Spectator Australia, October 28, 2020, at https://www.spectator.com.au/2020/10/
    scott-morrison-dismal-with-daniel-andrews-feeble-on-freedom/.

2   T. S. Eliot, (1927) [1925] *Poems 1909-1925*. London: Faber & Faber, 128.

3   See, for example, Andrew Swarbrick, (1988) *Selected Poems of T. S. Eliot*. Basingstoke
    and London: Macmillan, 45.

4   Robert Gottliebsen, 'Christine Holgate latest to pay a price for Australia Post's success'
    The Australian, October 23, 2020, at https://www.theaustralian.com.au/business/
    leadership/christine-holgate-latest-to-pay-a-price-for-australia-posts-success/news-st
    ory/4a4df8d65785d58b8aae2388d38d4c45.

5   Janet Albrechtsen, 'PM monsters a patsy but indulges a villain', *The Australian*, October
    27, 2020, at https://www.theaustralian.com.au/commentary/scott-morrison-
    monsters-australia-post-boss-christine-holgate-but-indulges-daniel-andrews/news-
    story/c72a025ac8513a065f7f2c54879a1fcc ('Albrechtsen').

6   Monica Wilkie, *Victims of Failure – how the COVID-19 policy response let down
    Australians*, Centre for Independent Studies, at https://www.cis.org.au/publications/
    analysis-papers/victims-of-failure-how-the-covid-19-policy-response-let-down-
    australians/.

7   Ibid, 6.

8   Transcript of Prime Minister's Media Conference of July 22, 2021, at https://www.
    pm.gov.au/media/press-conference-canberra-act-6.

9   Daniel McCulloch, 'Prime Minister Scott Morrison replies to religious leaders on
    coronavirus vaccine', 7 News, August 28, 2020, at https://7news.com.au//lifestyle/
    health-wellbeing/pm-replies-to-religious-leaders-on-vaccine-c-1272768.

10 Alison Xiao, 'Oxford University coronavirus vaccine has "ethical concerns", Sydney
    Archbishops warn followers', ABC News, August 24, 2020, at https://www.abc.net.
    au/news/2020-08-24/sydney-catholic-archbishop-warns-pm-against-coronavirus-
    vaccine/12588578.

11 See Steve Waterson, 'Covid vaccine segregation? This isn't 1950s Alabama', *The Australian*, September 18, 2021, at https://www.theaustralian.com.au/inquirer/covid-vaccine-segregation-this-isnt-1950s-alabama/news-story/b890cecfa550dca0387d7923186e7d57; and Rocco Loiacono, 'Vaccine segregation is an affront to liberty', *The Spectator Australia*, June 29, 2021, at https://www.spectator.com.au/2021/06/vaccine-segregation-is-an-affront-to-liberty/.

12 Sarah Newey, 'Herd immunity a 'mythical' goal that will never be reached, says Oxford vaccine head', *The Telegraph*, August 10, 2021, at https://www.telegraph.co.uk/global-health/science-and-disease/herd-immunity-mythical-goal-will-never-reached-says-oxford-vaccine/.

13 Tim Shipman, Caroline Wheeler and Oliver Wright, 'Covid vaccine passports scrapped for winter by Boris Johnson', *The Times*, September 12, 2021, at https://www.thetimes.co.uk/article/covid-vaccine-passports-scrapped-for-winter-by-boris-johnson-5g2fdb2zn.

14 Lily Zhou, 'UK to Repeal Emergency Powers Allowing Government to Shut Down Country', *The Epoch Times*, September 12, 2021, at https://www.theepochtimes.com/uk-to-repeal-emergency-powers-allowing-government-to-shut-down-country_3993319.html.

15 Michael Koziol, 'Scott Morrison warns against internal fight over free speech laws: "It doesn't create one job"', March 1, 2017, *Sydney Morning Herald* at https://www.smh.com.au/politics/federal/scott-morrison-warns-against-internal-fight-over-free-speech-laws-it-doesnt-create-one-job-20170301-gunoqu.html.

16 Chris Kenny, 'Four Corners: Fox News 'expose' shows same old script from the ABC', *The Australian*, August 24, 2021, at https://www.theaustralian.com.au/commentary/fox-news-expose-shows-same-old-script-from-the-abc/news-story/47600ded22bcc10fe9b4baa93a35541b.

17 Peta Credlin, 'Ending Canberra's 'toxic culture' will bring in more women: *Credlin* Sky News Australia, March 25, 2021, at https://www.skynews.com.au/australia-news/more-female-mps-is-important-but-not-a-panacea-peta-credlin/video/660ca996c54dd5f53bb4477e8c92cd5f. See also: Scott Morrison, An anthem for a nation that's one and free' *The Australian*, December 31, 2020, at https://www.theaustralian.com.au/commentary/an-anthem-for-a-nation   -thats-one-and-free/news-story/cc8d0546b6591c49dcbe3ac20c2e348f.

18 Tony Abbott, 'True conservatism is pragmatism based on values', *The Australian*, September 2, 2017, at https://www.theaustralian.com.au/nation/inquirer/true-conservatism-is-pragmatism-based-on-values/news-story/ba7af3d46b8e05350cca0f650b1962bf.

19 Ibid.

20 'Constitutional law professor argues Commonwealth can 'override' states on borders', Sky News Australia, November 18, 2020, at https://www.skynews.com.au/australia-news/constitutional-law-professor-argues-commonwealth-can-override-states-on-borders/video/bf6f8e2c26eeddc0c3f876dce29a1990.

21 Albrechtsen, above n. 5.

22 James Allan, 'Save the last dance for Scott', *The Spectator Australia*, March 27, 2021, at https://www.spectator.com.au/2021/03/save-the-last-dance-for-scott/.

23 Tom Switzer, 'Is Josh Frydenberg so wrong to invoke Thatcher and Reagan?', *Sydney Morning Herald*, July 29, 2020, at https://www.smh.com.au/national/is-josh-frydenberg-so-wrong-to-invoke-thatcher-and-reagan-20200729-p55gm8.html.

24 Ibid.

25 *Revenue Statistics 2020 – Australia*, Organisation for Economic Co-operation and Development, Centre for Tax Policy and Administration, at https://www.oecd.org/tax/revenue-statistics-australia.pdf.

26 Corporate Tax Statistics: Third Edition, Organisation for Economic Co-operation and Development, at https://www.oecd.org/tax/beps/corporate-tax-statistics-database.htm.

27 Matthew Cranston and Tom McIlroy, 'Australia among highest corporate tax collectors: OECD', *Australian Financial Review*, July 8, 2020, at https://www.afr.com/policy/economy/australia-among-highest-corporate-tax-collectors-oecd-20200708-p55a2v.

28 John Kehoe, 'NSW blows whistle on tax failing', *Australian Financial Review*, July 2, 2020, at https://www.afr.com/policy/tax-and-super/nsw-blows-whistle-on-tax-failings-20200701-p5584w.

29 Tony Makin, 'Wrong lessons in Covid response', *The Australian*, December 30, 2020, at https://www.theaustralian.com.au/commentary/wrong-lessons-in-covid-response/news-story/1d96a765b67bad148f4cfffe94e5dc72.

30 See generally Ian Hanke, 'Sorry ScoMo, but this is tepid tinkering with IR laws, not real reform', *The Spectator Australia*, December 11, 2020, at https://www.spectator.com.au/2020/12/sorry-scomo-but-this-is-tepid-tinkering-with-ir-laws-not-real-reform/.

31 Peta Credlin, 'PM's switch to net zero leaves us in dark', *The Australian*, October 13, 2021, at https://www.theaustralian.com.au/commentary/pms-switch-to-net-zero-leaves-us-indark/news-story/4b14f1b8ad9826294120c83f654adbda.

32 Steven Hamilton, 'A prayer, not a plan, for net zero', *Australian Financial Review*, October 27, 2021, at https://www.afr.com/policy/energy-and-climate/a-prayer-not-a-plan-for-net-zero-20211026-p5939u.

33 Credlin, above, n. 32.

34 'Net zero commitment is a 'death knell' of the Morrison government: *Credlin*, Sky News Australia, October 26, 2021, at https://www.skynews.com.au/opinion/alan-jones/net-zero-commitment-is-a-death-knell-of-the-morrison-government-credlin/video/705c520960ce70e9c47b40e824df0a9b.

35 'Morrison has 'blurred the lines' between Liberal and Labor parties', Sky News Australia, October 26, 2021, at https://www.skynews.com.au/opinion/alan-jones/morrison-has-blurred-the-lines-between-liberal-and-labor-parties/video/0dd0f5d325cbe28477e582a6afc0b287.

36 Charles Pier, 'The Coalition's climate stand: just like pissing in a wetsuit' *The Spectator Australia*, October 27, 2021, at https://spectator.com.au/2021/10/the-coalitions-climate-stand-just-like-pissing-in-a-wetsuit/.

ACKNOWLEDGEMENTS

There are several people who deserve our gratitude for helping us realise this project. We thank most sincerely Dave Pellowe, who worked unstintingly to get this work published in such a short space of time. Additionally, Dave has gone "the extra mile" in his promotional efforts. We also thank him for his patience with us. We express our gratitude to James Allan for providing the Foreword, and for his invaluable suggestions regarding the manuscript.

We are also extremely grateful to Rowan Dean for his promotional efforts and assistance. Rowan is such a steadfast supporter of conservatives. Without him, and others such as Roger Franklin, we wouldn't have a voice. This goes, too, for all the outlets that have published the pieces that form the basis of this critical reflection.

In this regard, it would be remiss of us not to mention the late Christian Kerr, former online editor of the *Spectator Australia*. Over the last few years, Christian was a constant source of encouragement and wise counsel. One of a kind, he became a firm friend, and his loss leaves a big void. May he rest in peace.

Finally to Judy, for her love and support, given always without hesitation.

ABOUT THE AUTHORS

Rocco Loiacono is a Senior Lecturer at Curtin University Law School, where he teaches in the areas of Property Law and Legal Research and Writing. In his capacity as a NAATI (National Accreditation Authority for Interpreters and Translators) Certified Translator (Italian>English), he also lectured for many years in the Masters of Translation Studies at the University of Western Australia. After graduating with a combined Law and Languages (First Class Honours) degree, he practised as a lawyer for ten years, most of that time at Clayton Utz, one of Australia's largest law firms. Rocco received the award of his PhD from the University of Western Australia in 2014, which focussed on the translation difficulties arising from the differences that exist between continental legal systems and the English common law, and he has published widely on this topic in peer-reviewed journals of translation, linguistics and law. In October 2017 he was invited to speak at the launch of the *Recommended National Standards for Working with Interpreters in Australian Courts and Tribunals* at Old Parliament House in Canberra, alongside the then Minister for Multicultural Affairs, Senator the Hon. Zed Seselja and the then Chief Justice of Western Australia, the Hon. Wayne Martin. Rocco has always had an interest in politics, fundamental freedoms and the rule of law, and contributes regularly on these matters in *The Spectator Australia, Quadrant Online, The Epoch Times* and *The Australian,* as well as authoring a chapter in *Fundamental Rights in the Age of Covid-19,* Connor Court Publishing, 2021.

Augusto Zimmermann is Professor and Head of Law at Sheridan Institute of Higher Education in Perth, Western Australia. He is also the Founder and President of the Western Australian Legal Theory Association, the Founder and Editor-in-Chief of *The Western Australian Jurist*, an Elected Fellow at the International Academy for the Study of the Jurisprudence of the Family, and a former Vice-President of the Australasian Society of Legal Philosophy. From 2012 to 2017 Professor Zimmermann served as a Law Reform Commissioner with the Law Reform Commission of Western Australia. He was also the Murdoch University Law School's Associate Dean for Research (2009-2012). While working at that university, he was awarded the 2012 Vice Chancellor's Award for Excellence in Research, and two Law School Dean's Research Awards, in 2010 and 2011. He served on numerous academic bodies at Murdoch, including: the Research Degree and Scholarships Committee; the Vice Chancellor's Awards and Citations Committee; the Academic Council's Freedom of Speech in Policies and Procedures Advisory Group; and the Academic Staff Promotions Advisory Committee. In January 2015, Professor Zimmermann was invited by the Tasmanian Chief Justice to address the 'Opening of the Legal Year' in that state. His address was attended by the Governor of Tasmania, the State Premier, the Leader of the Opposition, the State Attorney-General, and Tasmanian judges, and lawyers. He is generally recognised as a fierce advocate for free speech and the Rule of Law, Professor Zimmermann is the author of numerous articles on these topics, contributing, inter alia, for a seminal book about the Rule of Law edited by the President of the American Bar Association. He is the author/co-author/editor/co-editor of numerous academic articles and books, including *Fundamental Rights in the Age of Covid-19*, Connor Court Publishing, 2021; *No Offence Intended: Why 18C is Wrong*, Connor Court Publishing, 2016; *Christian Foundations* *of the Common Law*, 3 Volumes, Connor Court Publishing, 2018; *Global Perspectives on Subsidiarity*, Springer, 2014; and *Western Legal Theory: History, Concepts and Perspectives*, LexisNexis, 2013.

www.ingramcontent.com/pod-product-compliance
Lightning Source LLC
Chambersburg PA
CBHW060454280326
41933CB00014B/2750